£16·95
METT

D1461432

National Institute of Economic and Social
   Research
Policy Studies Institute
Royal Institute of International Affairs

Joint Studies in Public Policy 9

EDUCATION AND
ECONOMIC PERFORMANCE

National Institute of Economic and Social
Research
Policy Studies Institute
Royal Institute of International Affairs

Joint Studies in Public Policy

STEERING COMMITTEE

National Institute of Economic and Social
   Research
Policy Studies Institute
Royal Institute of International Affairs

Joint Studies in Public Policy 9

EDUCATION AND ECONOMIC PERFORMANCE

Edited by
G. D. N. Worswick

Gower

Published by
Gower Publishing Company Limited,
Gower House,
Croft Road,
Aldershot, Hants GU11 3HR,
England

and

Gower Publishing Company,
Old Post Road,
Brookfield,
Vermont 05036,
U.S.A.

Acknowledgement
The Steering Committee gratefully acknowledge the support of the Economic and Social Research Council which financed the conference and the research and editorial work involved in the preparation of this book.

ISBN 0 566 00848 3

Phototypesetting by Swanston Typesetting, Derby
Printed in Great Britain by Biddles Ltd, Guildford, Surrey

Contents

Contributors and Participants

Professor Mark Blaug, University of London, Institute of Education

Professor Leonard Cantor, University of Technology, Loughborough

Professor Sir Charles Carter, Policy Studies Institute

Sir Hugh Ford, Sir Hugh Ford Associates Limited

D. R. Glynn, Chief Economist, Peat, Marwick, Mitchell & Company, formerly Economic Director, CBI

Professor Alain d'Iribarne, Laboratoire d'Economie et de Sociologie du Travail

Roy Jackson, Trades Union Congress

Ian S. Jones, Research Officer, National Institute of Economic and Social Research

Professor M. Kogan, Brunel University

Stuart Maclure, Times Educational Supplement

Professor M. Peston, Queen Mary College, University of London

Professor Neville Postlethwaite, University of Hamburg

Professor S. J. Prais, Senior Research Fellow, National Institute of Economic and Social Research

T. J. Russell, Coombe Lodge Further Education College, Bristol

David Stanton, Employment Market Research Unit, Department of Employment

Dr. W. Taylor, Principal, University of London

Professor Gareth L. Williams, School of Education, University of Lancaster

G. D. N. Worswick, CBE, FBA, Consultant, National Institute of Economic and Social Research

Other Participants

A.J.C. Britton	D. Morris
W.W. Daniel	P. Oppenheimer
Professor P.J.H.H. Gosden	Sir Richard O'Brien
C. Hayes	M. Quinlan, CB
Professor R.M. Lindley	Professor D.K. Stout
Mrs J. Marquand	M. Tomlinson
D. Marsden	R. Walker

Preface

This book is the ninth in the series of Joint Studies in Public Policy and is based on a conference organised by the National Institute of Economic and Social Research, on behalf of the three participating Institutes, on 12 and 13 June, 1984. The origin of this Conference was the work undertaken at the ESRC Designated Centre in Comparative Industrial Structure and Efficiency under the direction of Dr. S.J. Prais. Some of that research is represented here and Dr. Prais himself was largely responsible for the structure of this Conference. The papers and the written comments of discussants are printed in three groups, each of which is followed by a summary of the discussion at the conference. We start off with Sir Charles Carter's paper on the implications for policy and research. These observations, together with the summary of the discussion which followed them can be read as the immediate conclusions of the conference. The remaining papers are printed in the order in which they were considered.

The Economic and Social Research Council financed this conference and its support is gratefully acknowledged. Thanks are also due to the Secretary of the National Institute, Mrs K. Jones, for conference arrangements and editorial help; to Mrs Fran Robinson for preparing the papers for the printers; to Anne Stewart for compiling the index; to Ian Jones for preparing the summary of the discussions and to the Nuffield Foundation for enabling us to meet at Nuffield Lodge.

GDNW
London, July 1984

1 Introduction
by G. D. N. Worswick

Economic performance

It has been common knowledge among economists for a very long time that labour productivity in British manufacturing industry was far lower than in the United States, of the order of one half. This fact was widely publicised at the end of the second world war, but there were some suggestions that we need not take the difference too much to heart. The United States economy, it was said, was very much larger than ours and had a different structure. It disposed of a much wider range of natural resources. Its consumers were more willing to accept mass production at the expense of quality, and so on and so forth. It was not difficult to find reasons for complacency, the more so since other European countries' economies appeared to be in much the same boat as ourselves. However, in the last quarter of a century not only has there been little narrowing of the gap in labour productivity in manufacturing between Britain and the United States but we have been overtaken by most European countries as well. German productivity, for instance, overtook that of Britain around 1960 and by the late 1970s was already one-third higher. Productivity is less difficult to measure and to compare in manufacturing than in other parts of the economy, notably services, but there is little reason to think that relatively poor performance in the manufacturing sector is significantly offset by superior performance in other sectors. Since the resource endowments of the British and German economies are not dissimilar, this was a result which could not so easily be ignored.

Education and the economy interact with one another. The state of the economy influences the volume of resources which will be made available for education and training. In the other direction, the volume and also the content of schooling, higher education and vocational training are likely to have effects, favourable or otherwise, on future economic performance. Early enthusiasts for the 'economics of education' may have muddied the waters somewhat by overemphasising a positive association found between the volume of education, measured by the number of years spent at school and at university, and the level of income. We have no more reason to believe that all education is favourable to economic growth than that all scientific research will raise future national income. Some education may well be hostile to economic growth, though not necessarily to be opposed on this ground alone since other values may outweigh economic efficiency. In this book we are concerned almost wholly with the line from schooling and vocational training to subsequent economic performance. Higher education and research are just as important in this regard, but we have excluded them because the ground has been covered many times, whereas there has been comparatively little discussion of schooling and vocational training.

Our purpose has been to bring together education experts and economists to discuss the influence of education on economic performance. There are powerful reasons making for a high degree of specialisation in scientific enquiry and the social sciences are no exception. Specialists in one field may be quite unaware of matters taken for granted by everyone in another field. Economists eavesdropping on discussions between education experts may sometimes be surprised at some of the presuppositions about economics and the economy which they hear. Equally, educationists may react strongly against some of the ways in which economists look at things.

The questions which were put before the conference originated mainly with economists. Much research has been undertaken to find explanations of the slower growth of productivity in Britain, and there have been attempts to quantify the respective contributions to growth of different factors such as labour, capital, industrial organisation, education, foreign trade and so on. Though few would believe it possible to say with precision just how much gain in economic performance could be achieved by improvements in schooling and vocational training, equally few economists would question their importance in the longer run.

Vocational training

In the past much has been made of the influence of higher education and particularly of the numbers qualifying in degrees in science and technology. In this respect Britain is not all that much behind. In the late 1970s the proportion of the British labour force with degree level qualifications was 5.5 per cent compared with 7.1 per cent in Germany. But if we turn to intermediate qualifications, such as apprenticeships, City and Guilds certificates, full secretarial qualifications and the like, only 30 per cent of the British labour force were so qualified compared with some 60 per cent in Germany. In fact nearly two-thirds of the British labour force are without any vocational qualifications at all compared with only one-third in Germany, and work done so far suggests that many other countries are nearer to the German proportion than the British.

It is not only in the amount of provision that the German system has differed from the British. Besides its comparative universality its outstanding features have been its formality, the inclusion of regular practical tests and examinations, the insistence on mathematics as a core subject, and the way in which the training system appears to grow naturally out of the school system. By contrast, the British have provided less training and what they have provided is often informal. There may have been no examinations at all and links with the school system are altogether more tenuous. Day release in Britain, for instance, has been limited and on a voluntary basis. The sole experiment in compulsory day release, the Rugby continuation school which was in existence from 1920 to 1965, was started to provide general and not vocational training, though the course was later modified in a vocational direction.

The differences between Germany and Britain are the starting point for many different routes of further enquiry. What about other countries, for instance? Professor d'Iribarne outlines developments in France in the past two decades. Then we must remember that the economic environment has changed dramatically in recent years. On the one hand the system of training, such as it was a few years ago, has had to respond to the biggest recession since the 1930s. In Britain this had led to the virtual abandonment by employers of the traditional apprenticeship system. On the other hand the Government, especially through the Manpower Services Commission, has launched a new training initiative: in particular the Youth Training Scheme (YTS) begun in 1983 was able to report at the beginning of this year that 320,000 young people had begun training under YTS. Mr Russell's comparison of recent developments in Britain and Germany is of the greatest interest here.

The White Paper, 'Training for Jobs', of January 1984 contains a number of proposals for the next steps in modernising vocational training in Britain. But before we come to consider plans for the future, it is worthwhile asking why Britain's provision, until very recently, has been so meagre. Ian Jones, in his chapter on skill formation and pay relativities, gives an economist's answer. There is clear evidence that in Britain in the past the supply of potential trainees considerably exceeded the number of apprenticeship vacancies, whereas in Germany there was, over many years, an approximate balance of demand and supply of trainees. Why this difference? The economist's answer is found by inspecting pay relativities, in particular the difference in pay between trainees and other workers of the same age, and the difference between the rates of pay of skilled and unskilled adult workers. Jones finds that there are no great differences between the relative pay of skilled and unskilled adult workers in Britain as compared with

Germany or Switzerland. On the other hand there is a very striking difference in the relative pay of trainees with respect to adult workers in Britain and Germany. It also turns out that British apprentices, on average, earn roughly the same as non-apprentices, while German apprentices earn a half or less.

In the economist's terminology, the imbalance between the supply of and demand for trainees is a clear instance of market failure. But why has this particular part of the labour market failed or been made to fail? In whose interest has it been to pay trainees far more than seems necessary and certainly a much higher proportion of the adult wage than is required in some other countries with workplace-based training systems and so to restrict training? If trainee wages fell to market-clearing levels, would this be sufficient to produce the socially optimal quantity of training? Or is a payroll subsidy, such as the YTS currently provides, necessary to any workplace-based training system? If so, can we learn from German experience? There, an approximate balance between supply and demand in the training market has been achieved, even in the face of a greatly increased supply of trainees in the late 1970s, without the need for any substantial measures of payroll subsidy.

Education

Whatever the merits of such vocational training as was available, the fact is that until very lately the only preparation for the world of work for the great majority of young people was compulsory schooling, and even if, in the foreseeable future, there is some kind of further educational or training provision for everyone between the ages of 16 and 19 excluding, of course, those proceeding to higher education, the type and quality of schooling will still have a great bearing upon future economic performance. Two of the most commonly expressed dissatisfactions with the present state of affairs concern standards and the alleged irrelevance of the curriculum. It is not so commonly noticed that the two criticisms do not necessarily reinforce one another. If children are being taught the wrong things it is not obviously to the advantage of the economy that they should be taught them better.

In the matter of standards, highly coloured personal impressions are rife and serious scientific study hard to come by, but we do well to begin with the account by Professor Postlethwaite of the results of work done by the International Association for the Evaluation of Educational Achievement (IEA) and the comparison of results in mathematics tests in Germany and England made by Dr Prais. The 1978 IEA data concern science and reading comprehension; improvements here will surely be favourable to economic performance. Nor is there likely to be serious dispute about the importance of mathematics in a world of rapidly advancing technology. But apparently the comparison is not straightforward. Prais shows that at the top academic levels mathematical attainments in England are better than in Germany; it is among the less able that attainment in England is so much lower. If mathematics teaching resources are taken as given, would the economy benefit if some of them were switched from the more able to the less able children? This is an economist's question; but it is still a question for all that.

Prais' comparisons with Germany also raise other important issues for educational policy. The German school system is selective. At ages 10–12 most children are divided into three types of school: academic, technical and vocational. The British have set themselves against selection at such an early age, although they stick firmly with it when it comes to higher education. Obviously the move to comprehensive schooling cannot be the cause of Britain's comparatively poor levels of attainment in mathematics since the tests referred to by Prais were administered in 1963. But has the move to a comprehensive schooling system improved or worsened Britain's relative performance? Closely associated with the three types of school is the use in Germany of a curriculum specific to each level – leading in turn to a school-leaving certificate based on average attainment across a broad range of about ten subjects. For those in the main schools, catering roughly for the bottom half of the ability range, this school-leaving certificate is in turn the 'entry gate' to apprenticeship training. This is all in great contrast to the incoherence of British educational provision in respect of the needs of youngsters in the bottom half of the ability range.

In his survey of productivity and educational values Professor Taylor notes the persistence into the postwar world of the conflict between traditional educational values and the claims of economic growth. In advocating the merits of the stationary state, John Stuart Mill observed that: '...the best state for human nature is that in which, while no-one is poor, no-one desires to be richer, nor has any cause to fear being thrust back, by the efforts of others to push themselves.' Such sentiments are, one suspects, not uncongenial to many of those who devote their lives to teaching the young. The economists have to make and to re-make the case for the advantages of greater economic efficiency. And they are not well placed to do it at a time of mass unemployment. If we put this last objection aside as taking too short-run a view, can the economist and the industrialist specify the optimum curriculum to promote productivity? If they can, how can it be brought about? These are the issues which are addressed by Stuart Maclure in his chapter on the responsiveness of the education system to change.

Implications for policy and research

In preparing for the conference out of which this book has arisen, it became apparent that there are some things about which quite a lot is known and others very little, and where new research is needed. Great new experiments are being undertaken in YTS and Technical and Vocational Education Initiative (TVEI), for instance. Will the former be judged in ten years' time simply as a palliative for youth unemployment, and the latter seen to prove once more that to bring about change, pure reason is not enough and must be backed by money? An effort must be made to monitor the changing scene.

Sir Charles Carter was invited to introduce the final session on the implications of the conference for future policy and research. He makes the point initially that the whole approach to these questions would be transformed if it were made a *requirement* that all young people after completion of compulsory schooling should undertake some recognised programme of education, or training, whether full-time or part-time in conjunction with paid employment. There is little doubt that the introduction of such a requirement would greatly reduce what Professor Cantor has characterised in his chapter as the current incoherence of British provision for the 16-19 year old age group. Linked to the specification of certain basic educational attainments as conditions of entry, it could also act as a major stimulant to the improvement of standards especially of the bottom half in our secondary schools. Yet difficult questions would remain to be settled, such as the level of financial assistance to be given to young people, which would have an important influence on the distribution of training activities between workplace-based and other types of provision.

Sir Charles's contribution also introduces a note of caution regarding the time-scale necessary to achieve significant changes to current arrangements. Even if links between education, training provision, and economic performance can be established, the process of developing the necessary consensus for change may well be lengthy. Moreover, it would still be many years before any such changes yielded discernible results, by which time new problems not yet foreseen may have presented themselves.   The world will not obligingly cease to rotate while the policy-makers study the results of their endeavours.

Part 1 Implications for Policy and Research

2 Implications for Policy and Research
by Charles Carter

I will assume it to be a conclusion of the conference that the economic performance of Britain may be impaired by faults of tradition and practice in its education system; and that, despite a number of policy initiatives in the last few years (well summarised by Professor Cantor), there is need to do more. Writing two years ago, John Pinder and I summarised the problem as follows: 'Our present educational system is designed to provide large numbers of people who are unskilled or who perform unchanging routine skills: and the world no longer needs many such people in its advanced economies'[1]. However, this formulation is deficient in one important respect. We are all of us educated by a great variety of influences, formal and informal: family, friends, the media, private study, hobbies, training at work, the experience of overcoming problems at work and in private life. The school and the college are only contributors, and perhaps only minority contributors, to the total of education. In talking of the 'educational system', therefore, we should really mean the total set of influences which have developed the qualities of the young; in particular, it should *not* be supposed that schools and colleges should necessarily develop skills capable of being slotted immediately into the requirements of the economy. Part of that task belongs to employers, and can better be performed within the incentives of a work situation.

Clarity of thought is impeded by the almost universal habit of thinking of skill in terms of the minority employer, manufacturing industry. It is almost certain that the manpower requirements of manufacturing will continue to decline, and that new service occupations will appear, with their own skill requirements. People find it easier to imagine future skills in manufacturing – moving, say, from manually controlled machine tools to numerical control and then to the supervision of robots – than to imagine how the larger non-manufacturing sector will develop. Indeed, to a large extent we must be ignorant; and it follows that an essential element of the preparation of the young must be to provide flexibility of adaptation to unknown future situations. That in turn implies a need for effective training in a range of *basic* skills; because a first job requires little numeracy or little skill in verbal expression, it must not be assumed that these qualities will be of no significance in ten or in twenty years' time.

By reason of inborn or acquired mental or physical defect, society necessarily contains a number of people incapable of obtaining, or of exercising to the full, skills of value in the market. We are used to the idea of providing sheltered employment for those with severe disablement, so that they can be assured that they are wanted by society; but a lot of other people who can obtain no skill qualification have traditionally taken unskilled jobs, which are now fast disappearing. It is therefore important to establish how many young people are 'ineducable' (in the sense of not being *able*, however well taught, to acquire marketable skills), and how many are 'educable but not educated'. The latter group is almost certainly much the larger, but there is need for more research on the size of the 'ineducable' group, and on means of identifying them, so that we may make proper provision of sheltered employment for them.

My further proposals for policy and research will relate to the great majority, who are certainly capable of making a contribution in a modern economy but some of whom fail to get the necessary preparation. I applaud the efforts being made, particularly by the Manpower Services Commission, to improve things; but the scale of the problem, as revealed by the comparisons with Germany and other countries, suggests to me that we must go beyond providing *opportunities* – which tend to be ignored by just that group which is most at risk. I suggest, therefore, that we should move as quickly as we can to a universal training *requirement*, which would extend the existing requirement of compulsory education. Specifically, I propose that there should be a requirement, to be fulfilled between the ages of 15 and 19, of further education and training equivalent to two years full-time; and that this requirement should be capable of being fulfilled, or over-fulfilled, in various ways:

(a) by continuing at school, for example to take A-level examinations, but with a requirement that the vocational content of courses should be increased;
(b) by entering full-time or part-time further education, but with a similar requirement of vocational content. (The proposal is phrased as 'two years after 15', rather than 'one year after 16', to allow the transfer from school to take place at 15 – the minimum leaving age in Germany – where appropriate;
(c) by an approved apprenticeship or similar training by an employer, supplemented by further education as appropriate; and
(d) by a combination of these.

The effect of this would be to remove the choice of having *no* relevant training; obviously one would hope to develop new types of 'modern apprenticeship' which would provide, for much larger numbers than at present, training more substantial than the minimum requirement. It would be a productive use of taxes to subsidise employers' costs heavily in providing training of approved standard; and the payment of the subsidy could be linked to the maintenance of the standard. A further incentive might be a 'training tax' on all employers, recoverable by those who provide training of an appropriate standard.

There would remain, however, problems abut basic schooling; and here there is a dilemma. The diversity of British education is a strength; indeed, more diversity and experiment would be desirable. The opposition of educators to central control, which might produce a dull uniformity, is therefore justified (even though it sometimes rests on a myth about what happens in France). But education is a fashion industry, and often seems to adorn its garments with the latest gimmicks and accessories without having enough concern for the basic quality of the underlying cloth. It also maintains and defends a system of specialisation in secondary education which the example of other countries shows to be unnecessary. I believe, therefore, that the diversity of method and approach, to be encouraged in education, has to be exercised within constraints which will require effective teaching of basic skills of literacy, communication and numeracy (and that means giving enough time to them), and the mandatory teaching of a range of core subjects, with criterion-referenced examinations, throughout secondary education. This is of course in line with Government thinking, but it is not clear to me how the Department of Education and Science proposes to proceed beyond exhortation to mandatory requirements, as I believe it must.

The imposition of such a requirement would, however, rapidly show up some other weaknesses. A leading one is the parlous state of mathematics teaching, some of which is undertaken by teachers with no proper qualification. There are other shortage subjects, too; and, as an economist, I find it astonishing that we suppose that such difficulties can be solved while ignoring market forces. Differentiation of teacher salaries, so that those whose skills are valuable elsewhere can be retained in teaching, seems to me essential. Another problem lies in the nature of teacher education. Bernard Shaw's dictum, 'He who can, does. He who cannot, teaches', is rather cruel, but there is ground for concern about the separation of the teaching ethos from the world of industry and commerce (about which some teachers are, indeed, contemptuous), and about the possibility of passing from school to college and then back to teach in school with no exposure to other employment. I suggest for consideration that the normal recruitment to teacher training should be of adult students who have had experience of other kinds; and that the Government should fund a substantial programme for the release of teacher trainers to work outside education, and for in-service courses which extend the range of their knowledge about that outside world.

It is possible – and I think likely – that the quality of basic preparation needed cannot be provided within present expectations about the number of hours of schooling in the year, and the amount of work to be done. In other words, we may not be asking the young to work hard enough; international comparisons suggest that they get off rather lightly. Some school teachers, and (in my observation) rather a lot of teachers in further and higher education, also allow themselves rather modest expectations about hours of work. I suggest as a subject for research the study of an optimum load on learners, and of the workload of teachers in relation to that of other occupations. It is also for consideration whether the effectiveness of the teaching process would not be increased by a greater use of ancillaries. In fact, all aspects of the 'productivity' of teaching need to be investigated; the profession too easily seems to convey a dedication to reducing its productivity, and there will be need to alter this thinking if the necessary extra costs of a proper education and training programme are to be acceptable to the taxpayer.

I conclude with a further proposal for research. As earlier contributors have made clear, our problem in this conference is a venerable one; it has been talked about for many generations, and many worthy experiments have been tried. (For instance, more than half a century ago, I lived in a town which had compulsory day release for further education). Maybe the latest initiatives will get us there at last – and it is certainly important that they do not rely exclusively on the traditional educational agencies; but the prudent will suppose that the obstacles to change lie deep in the nature of British society, and that they will not be easily shifted until they are better understood. I suggest, therefore, a programme of research on 'Why things, widely and long asserted to be sensible and urgent, do not happen'.

Reference
[1] Carter, C. and Pinder, J., *Policies for a Constrained Economy*, Heinemann, 1982, p.105.

Summary of the Discussion

The conference considered the implications of its discussion for public policy and for research into training and education matters.

Policy

Not surprisingly, in the light of the differences of opinion both on facts and their interpretation revealed among the contributors to the conference, no unanimous recommendations emerged from the discussions.

Postlethwaite's suggestion for the creation of a single national centre for curriculum development (linked to what he felt was the need for a much greater uniformity in the school curriculum) was opposed by some speakers on the ground that there were many roads to Rome and that what was needed was more and not less experimentation with syllabuses.

The proposals for the effective universalisation of programmes of training and further education for the 15/16–18/19 age group put forward by both Cantor (by means of an extension of the YTS to two years) and Carter (through the introduction of a universal training and further education requirement), were briefly discussed. There was widespread support for the view that the YTS should not be allowed to become a refuge for those least likely to obtain employment; at the same time, the scheme should not stand in the way of greatly expanded provision of more skill intensive forms of initial training. One issue which these proposals raised was whether, given constraints on public expenditure, it would be in the best interests of the young people themselves to concentrate state provision on their initial training at a time when their own preferences had not been clearly formed. Perhaps more resources should be devoted to providing opportunities for adult training and retraining. French ideas on *alternance*, referred to by d'Iribarne, provided a possible framework of reference here.

The inconclusive nature of the discussion of specific policy proposals reflected the difficulty of establishing, in the present state of knowledge, a clear line between the education and training of the labour force on the one hand and economic performance on the other. Until it is more systematically established that apparent British deficiencies, for example, in the mathematical attainments of school-children or in the provision of craft and technician training in the 16-19 year old age group are damaging to economic performance, there will be an inevitable reluctance on the part of the education and training systems to change their practices so as to alter these aspects of their performance.

Research

These considerations were reflected in some of the recommendations for further research which emerged from the discussions. Thus there was widespread support for the view that the comparisons of labour force qualifications and training systems should be extended to cover other successful economies (such as Japan) as well as Germany and also some less successful economies. This would be complementary to further research, probably at the level of the individual manufacturing plant, aimed at identifying the effects of differences in labour force qualifications on economic performance, and to further examination of the economic implications of the alleged 'over-training' in some occupations which occurred in Germany.

It was also argued that discussions of British performance were too narrowly focussed on the manufacturing sector; more needed to be known about the extent of international differences in training provision in the non-manufacturing sectors of the economy and of their effects on economic performance.

In the light of the disagreements revealed in the discussions on the effectiveness with which the needs of the economy were transmitted to the education and training 'markets', there was general support for research designed to illuminate the decision-making processes on both the supply and demand sides of the markets concerned.

Despite the disagreements about the significance of the actual results of the international comparisons of educational attainment presented to the conference, it was widely agreed that this type of work could provide a useful benchmark against which to assess the relative performance of the British education system and therefore should be actively pursued. Although much was being spent in Britain on performance measurement (particularly at the Assessment of Performance Unit (APU)) there were doubts as to whether the results of this work were being adequately disseminated.

It was suggested that there should be more research into what might be called the cost-effectiveness of different styles of teaching. There was also a recommendation for further work by economists on the public financing issues in training and education, in particular, what it is appropriate for government to subsidise.

Finally, the conference heard a plea for the development of appropriate financial incentives to encourage multi-disciplinary research and economists present were reminded of the substantial volume of research into educational policy, administration and economics conducted within the world of education, registers of which should be carefully consulted before embarking on 'path-breaking' projects.

Part 2 Training

3 A Coherent Approach to the Education and Training of the 16-19 Age Group
by Leonard Cantor

The first question to be answered is 'What do we understand by the 16-19 age group?' A precise definition and one which will be adopted for the purposes of this chapter is that it comprises all 16 year olds who have reached statutory school-leaving age (therefore excluding those who have reached the chronological age of 16 but who have not achieved the statutory school-leaving age) and all 17 and 18 year olds. As table 3.1 shows, this group for England and Wales comprised almost two-and-a-half million youngsters in January 1983, of whom 41.8 per cent were receiving some form of continuing education, 28.8 per cent were employed with no form of study and 29.4 per cent were unemployed. In the time that has elapsed since then, the percentage of unemployed youngsters has grown and one estimate suggested that in the autumn of 1983 half of the country's young people under 18 were out of work [7] although this total includes a greater seasonal element of school-leaving than the January figures in table 3.1

Table 3.1   The 16–19 age group[a], England and Wales, January 1983

	000s	Per cent
Stayed on at school	443	17.8
In higher education	81	3.2
In full-time and sandwich non-advanced further education	287	11.5
In employment with day release	188	7.5
In other part-time day study	45	1.8
In employment with no day study	718	28.8
Unemployed	730[b]	29.4
Total	2,492	100.0

Source: Department of Education and Science.

[a] Comprises all 16 year olds above statutory school-leaving age, with all 17 and 18 year olds.

[b] Of whom 230 were on Youth Opportunities Programmes.

In recent years, the needs of this age group have increasingly become the focus of national attention, so much so that they were the subject of keen political discussion in the run-up to the 1983 general election. There are several reasons for this growing concern. Firstly, the increasing maturity of young people, together with the lowering of the age of adulthood so that adult wages are paid at 18, have focussed attention on the problem of trainee wages for the 16-19 age group and the desirability of an obligatory training period. Secondly, the demographic changes which will shortly bring about a sharp decline in the size of the 16-19 population have emphasised the need to rationalise the provision of education and training. Thirdly, the last few years have witnessed a national debate about the curricular needs of the age group, particularly in regard to courses of vocational preparation. This debate has been partly occasioned by the growth in our secondary schools and technical colleges of a group of pupils who are increasingly staying on in full-time education, usually for one year, in the hope of improving their examination results and thus enhancing their job prospects. Unlike the traditional sixth former who is studying for A levels, they are mostly of an academic standard equivalent to CSE grades 2 to 4; they are predominantly female, though this characteristic is beginning to change with the decline in apprenticeships; and, being anxious to acquire marketable skills, they mostly take an 'instrumental' view of education. Fourthly, there are the 'industrial' demands, brought about by technological developments, for a better trained and more adaptable workforce, demands which have in part resulted in a re-evaluation of the traditional apprenticeship system. Finally, in some ways the most important catalyst of all has been the enormous growth in youth unemployment and the acute social and political problems it has brought in its train.

Present provision of education and training
The present provision of education and training for the 16-19 age group has grown up over a considerable period and is a mixture of well-established courses and new courses and programmes, which are to some extent *ad hoc* responses to events. If looked at from a curricular point of view, it can be broadly divided into three major categories.

Firstly, there are the 'academic' courses, particularly the General Certificate of Education (GCE), but also including the Certificate of Secondary Education (CSE) and the Certificate of Extended Education (CEE). These courses, of which approximately three-quarters are offered in secondary schools and one-quarter in non-advanced further education, emphasise cognitive development and, to a large extent, act as entry qualifications for higher education.

The second category are the 'traditional vocation or technical' courses which are almost entirely concentrated in non-advanced further education: the best examples of these are the programmes offered by the Business and Technician Examination Council (BTEC), the City and Guilds of London Institute (CGLI) and the Royal Society of Arts (RSA). These courses prepare young people for specific occupations, industries or professional associations as technicians, craftsmen, and secretaries and the syllabuses are therefore broadly speaking 'job-specific'. Many students in this category of courses have traditionally attended them on a part-time basis, especially those working as apprentices for CGLI craft qualifications. However, the number of apprenticeships has greatly diminished in recent years as a direct result of the industrial recession; in manufacturing, for example, they declined from a peak of 236,000 in 1968 to about 100,000 in 1982 [3]. Accompanying this decline has been a growing criticism of the apprenticeship programmes themselves. The Manpower Services Commission (MSC), for example, has declared that it is essential to modernise apprenticeship training by replacing time serving by new standards of training which ensure that all who reach them are accepted as competent. In 1981 the Government stated its intention of achieving by 1985 'recognised standards for all the main craft, technician and professional skills to replace time serving and age-restricted apprenticeships' [10].

The third category is one which has grown substantially only in the last six or seven years and is best described as 'vocational preparation'. It includes full-time pre-employment courses and programmes such as the Certificate of Pre-Vocational Education (CPVE) and the Technical and Vocational Education Initiative (TVEI) which are just beginning to establish themselves in secondary schools, the CGLI Certificate in Vocational Preparation (General) which is largely provided by further education colleges, and also programmes devised specifically or predominantly for unemployed youngsters such as the Youth Opportunities Programme (YOP) and its successor, the Youth Training Scheme (YTS), which are mainly provided 'on-the-job' by industry and business with some associated further education. This last category of courses and programmes has developed very largely in response to shrinking job opportunities and youth unemployment and, although they include a vocational orientation, are not job-specific like the second category of traditional vocational courses.

Both the CPVE and the TVEI are government inspired moves to nudge the secondary school curriculum in a vocational direction. CPVE, which began on a pilot basis in September 1983, is a new qualification designed by the Department of Education and Science (DES) for young people 'usually with modest examination achievement at 16-plus who have set their sights on employment rather than higher education, but have not yet formed a clear idea of the kind of job they might tackle successfully, or are not yet ready to embark on a specific course of vocational education or training' [5]. The course consists of a common core and options. The former, occupying nearly two thirds of the course time, includes English, mathematics, some science and technology and their application, careers education and guidance, and studies designed to give a broad understanding of citizenship and its responsibilities. The latter are designed to meet the particular needs of three categories of students: those whose vocational commitment is uncertain; those who want to work in factories or service industries; and those who want to go into offices or shops. The courses will be offered mainly in schools and the DES originally expected that about 80,000 students would eventually enrol on them, though this now seems unduly optimistic.

Towards the end of 1982, the MSC announced that a scheme to promote technical and vocational education in secondary schools would be introduced on a pilot basis from September 1983. The scheme, funded and administered by the MSC, would apply to students aged 14-18 and would start with 14-16 year olds in a limited number of local authority areas, chosen on the quality of their applications to the MSC and on geographical distribution. In broad terms, TVEI aims to shape the education of 14-18 year old young people so that they are better equipped to enter the world of business and industry, so that they acquire a more direct appreciation of the practical application of the qualifications for which they are working, and so that they are given the opportunity for direct contact and planned work experience with local industry and business. In its first year of operation, 1983-4, fourteen different schemes have emerged from individual authorities involving a total of 4,000 young people in 105 schools. Although each scheme varies in detail, they have certain features in common. They include major subject areas such as computing, information technology and business studies; they cater for students spanning the ability range; they are mostly school-based with some further education involvement which is likely to increase in the next year or two; and they all plan to integrate teaching and work experience in the second year of the programme.

It is still too early to evaluate the success or otherwise of TVEI but it seems to have had a beneficial effect on the schools concerned insofar as MSC money has enabled them to increase their facilities. It remains to be seen what effect TVEI programmes will have on the traditional academic sixth form once they are available beyond the age of 16. In the meantime, the MSC is pleased with progress so far and announced in the autumn of 1983 that another £80 million will be available for about 40 new experiments in the 1984-5 calendar year, thereby eventually involving just over half of the local education authorities in England and Wales.

The Youth Training Scheme began in September 1983. Welcomed in principle by all the major political parties, it started off with much goodwill but faces an uncertain future. The aims which it espouses are threefold; to provide participants with a better start in working and adult life through an integrated programme of training, education and work experience; to provide for the participating employers a better equipped young workforce; and to develop and maintain a more versatile, readily adaptable, highly motivated and productive work-force. To these ends the Scheme, which is voluntary, should be open to about 460,000 youngsters in its first year of operation, to cover both employed and unemployed young people, including those who are undergoing the first year of apprenticeship and other forms of training. It guarantees a full year's training for all those leaving school at minimum age and, where places are available, to those aged 17. The Scheme contains five major elements; a period of induction and assessment; the teaching of basis skills like numeracy; the development of practical competence in the use of tools and machinery and in some basic office occupations and the fostering of skills in communication; the provision of occupationally relevant education and training; guidance and counselling; and a record and review of each young person's progress.

Although YTS planned to accommodate approximately 460,000 youngsters in 1983-4, according to figures issued by the MSC, only about 354,000 had taken up places by March 1984 and the total is not likely to increase very much during the rest of the academic year. The shortfall of about one-third of the target numbers is attributed very largely to the fact that the Scheme has almost entirely failed to attract youngsters who are in employment. If YTS is to achieve its full potential, it must therefore persuade employers and others to use it for employed youngsters as well as those without jobs and as a permanent bridge between school and work for *all* young people. Another of the problems facing the Sceme is that its objectives are seen differently by different people [1]. Thus, trainers and educators see it primarily as a vehicle for teaching literacy and social and life skills and imparting the general flavour of work, whereas employers, and probably most trainees, see it essentially as job preparation. Indeed, one of the criticisms levelled at the MSC is that in respect of YTS it is developing vocational training schemes which bear little resemblance to the prevailing employment oppor-tunities and will do little therefore to bridge the gap between the aspirations of its young trainees and the realities of a declining wage labour market.

Future needs

Whatever the principles upon which YTS should be based, it is clear that much remains to be done before it is of a sufficiently high quality. In its first year of operation, most programmes have had to be put together in a hurry, with an inevitable loss of quality. In the next year or two an improvement in quality must be sought. This includes ensuring that the standards to be reached in core areas of training are carefully defined, for example along the lines of West German practice [11]. Accurate methods of assessing the performance of trainees must also be developed and work experience and off-the-job training in the further education colleges or elsewhere must be properly integrated.

To a large extent, the future success of YTS depends on two closely related developments: whether or not it provides young school leavers with good job opportunities and how it is accepted by them as a valid route to employment [12]. If the YTS can develop conditions and allowances which attract well-qualified school-leavers so that it is not regarded, as seems to be the case at present, as a second choice for those who cannot find employment, then most young people would enter the Scheme and remain on it for the year. If not, then attendance will fluctuate with the rise and fall of unemployment and it will fail to become the 'permanent bridge' between school and work which its proponents envisage. It is, of course, possible to ensure a full take-up of YTS and similar schemes by treating it in effect as a raising of the school-leaving age and making it illegal for young people under 17 to be employed. Another possibility, recently advocated by the Association of County Councils (ACC), would be to continue it into a second year so that it became in effect an apprenticeship scheme for all young school-leavers and was extended to areas outside those covered by the present formal apprenticeships scheme. The ACC also contends that provision of an integrated system of vocational education and training for the 16-19 age group requires responsibility at government level being vested in one department of state instead of being divided up as at present between the Department of Employment and the DES.

Some critics of the present education and training scheme argue that no radical improvement will be effected without more direct intervention by the Government. In this context, it is interesting to note that, in January 1984, the Department of Employment and the Department of Education and Science published jointly a White Paper [6] in which they state their intention of giving the MSC responsibility for spending about a quarter of the £800 million spent each year by local education authorities in England and Wales in work-related non-advanced further education. This shift in control is necessary, states the White Paper, to ensure that college provision of training and vocational education is more responsive to national and local employment needs and to allow important developments in job training to be carried through successfully. The latter include the adoption of a system of certification for young people on YTS and the provision of training courses needed for the economic health of the country, such as electronics and robotics.

The MSC currently accounts for just over 10 per cent of the £800 million spent by local education authorities in work-related further education by buying courses and services from the colleges. Under the new proposals, this share will more than double and the increased cost will be met from the general rate support grant to the local authorities so that they will have to reduce their spending by a commensurate amount. Inevitably, this proposal has aroused a considerable amount of criticism from the local authorities and is seen by many of them and by the teachers' unions as an unwarranted attack on the traditional education system, whereby responsibility for provision is devolved by the central authority (the DES) on the local education authorities and is a further indication of the increasingly 'dirigiste' policies adopted by the present government.

Whatever the rights and wrongs of these arguments, we clearly need to increase our stock of competent technicians and craftsmen to work in those industries and services which will change rapidly in response to technological developments and also in new ones which may be introduced following an economic recovery. However, the present situation of a declining wage labour market calls especially for the development of programmes which make young people aware that alternatives to unemployment do exist and that changing circumstances do present opportunities. Such programmes could teach them that they can secure some measure of control over their own circumstances by, for example, starting small enterprises which serve the specific needs of local communities. For all young people, however, it is essential to ensure that as many as possible of those who complete YTS and similar programmes obtain jobs. To this end, it is necessary for the training agencies, and MSC in particular, to develop more flexible programmes in which job search, preparation and placement are given a far greater emphasis [1].

Level of provision and distribution
This brief review of the present provision of education and training for the 16-19 age group has tried to demonstate something of the confusing variety of courses available and the lack of integration between them. However, it is not just that present provision is confusing, it is also inadequate in volume. Thus, before YTS came fully into operation, a considerably smaller percentage of those leaving school in this country received education and training than in our major industrial rivals in

Europe [9]. Moreover, among those who do continue with their education and training, there are considerable inequalities of opportunity: for example, the proportion of 16-19 year olds receiving full-time education is markedly lower among those of working class background than other socio-economic groups (table 3.2) and such programmes as they take up are often 'dead end' in character, inhibiting progression to more advanced courses. The nature of the provision itself is often fragmented and patchy, consisting sometimes of what is termed 'education', sometimes 'training', and sometimes both.

Table 3.2   Participation rates in full-time education of 16–19 year olds by socio-economic group of father, Great Britain, 1981

Socio-economic group of father	Participation rates, per cent
Semi-skilled and unskilled manual	18
Skilled manual and own account non-professional	25
Intermediate and junior non-manual	43
Employers and managers	45
Professional	66

Source: General Household Survey 1981, OPCS, HMSO, 1983, p.125.

Nationally, very little financial assistance is available to enable young people from poorer backgrounds to continue with their full-time education and such financial support as is forthcoming has been characterised as 'arbitrary, inadequate and unfair' [2]. In 1981-2, for example, 59 local education authorities provided approximately 27,500 awards, of which about half were given by only five authorities. The allowances varied from under £9 a week to under £3 a week, sums which contrasted most unfavourably with the £25 a week available to YOP trainees. As a consequence, families in financial difficulties are likely to put pressure on young people to leave full-time education in schools or further education colleges to take a place on a YTS programme or on the dole. One solution would be to institute a national mandatory scheme of educational maintenance allowances for all 16-18 year olds, possibly at the same level as YTS. In the run-up to the 1983 election, all the main opposition parties proposed their own versions of such a scheme but, understandably perhaps for a party in power, there are no signs of the present Conservative government adopting such a policy. Indeed, during 1983 the DES ruled out the establishment of a mandatory scheme of grants for young people staying on at school to take its new 17-plus qualification, the CPVE. As far as the further education colleges are concerned, they will undoubtedly be willing to take on to their courses at 17-plus youngsters who completed their year of YTS training. However, given the lack of financial incentive for youngsters to embark upon such courses, the take-up is likely to be relatively small.

Another characteristic feature of the provision of education and training for this age group has been the relative lack of opportunities for girls as compared to boys. This is very largely due to the neglect of training in the types of jobs which many girls have entered, such as clerical occupations and posts in the distributive trades and in unskilled factory work. As a result, while part-time day release in the late 1970s was taken up by approximately one-fifth of the young workforce, this was made up of about 35 per cent of the boys and only 8 per cent of the girls. Finally, the youth unemployment rate among ethnic minorities has grown faster than the unemployment rate of all young people. This partly reflects the high levels of unemployment in the major conurbations in which the ethnic minorities mainly live, Yorkshire and Humberside, the Midlands, the North West and London, where unemployment is compounded by other social and environmental problems [4].

Finally, any rational planning for 16-19 year olds must take into account the fact that the size of the age group is about to decline sharply. Although in 1984 the 16-19 age group is perhaps larger than it has ever been, it will drop by about a third in the next decade as a result of the decline in the birth rate in the 1970s. Even if more youngsters stay on in full-time education and there is a greater take-up of part-time day release, secondary schools and perhaps further education colleges will be faced by declining rolls. One response to this situation, likely to be widely adopted by local authorities, is the 'rationalisation' of provision by the establishment of tertiary colleges and sixth form colleges. Tertiary colleges, the sole providers of 16-19 education in the areas they serve, offer a wide range of courses, both academic and technical, catering for individual needs; they provide a more adult atmosphere than many schools and they represent a genuinely 'comprehensive' system catering for all abilities in one institution. In those areas, probably in the majority, where tertiary colleges are not established, the schools and colleges will still be faced by the need for major readjustments. Indeed, as we have seen, these readjustments are already taking place. In the secondary schools, the introduction of the CPVE and the pilot schemes of TVEI presage a growing orientation towards pre-vocational education and an increasing overlap with non-advanced further education. In the further education colleges, major changes have taken place in recent years to reflect and cater for a declining number of courses in the more traditional manufacturing industries accompanied by a growth in courses of training in new technologies, together with an increased demand for vocational education in the areas of business and allied services, especially in the public sector [8]. These courses have developed largely under the aegis of the Business and Technician Education Council (BTEC). At the same time, the colleges have greatly expanded their provision of vocational preparation courses, as a direct consequence of youth unemployment and mainly in response to initiatives by the MSC.

These rapid changes have imposed considerable strains on the education service and, in particular, on the teachers of the 16-19 age group. The increasing provision of courses of vocational preparation has brought specific problems in its train, especially for the colleges of further education. As we have seen, many of the programmes have come into being as a reaction to a crisis and, initially at least, have sacrificed quality to urgency. Most of the young people for whom programmes such as YTS are intended come from the lower socio-economic backgrounds and often have very modest educational attainment and an antipathy towards learning. The staff in the colleges teaching these courses have become much more heterogeneous than hitherto and include industrial trainers and tutors, as well as further education lecturers. If these new programmes are to achieve a high standard then a major programme of staff development is required, based on effective collaboration beween industrial training, further education and secondary schools. The need for such a programme has evoked a partial response from the DES which, towards the end of 1983, announced that £3 million would be made available in the financial year 1984-5 for staff development for further education teachers undertaking training in support of pre-vocational education, particularly YTS and CPVE.

The need for a comprehensive system
This review of the provision of education and training for the 16-19 age group and the problems associated with it has sought to direct attention to the need for a comprehensive system based on an integrated approach. Such a system would both enable us to increase our output of skilled young people to meet the needs of industry and business and also to provide education and training for the rest of the age group who, having left school, do not enter full-time occupation and for whom there is no employment.

Although there is some evidence of a correlation between increased and improved provision of education and training on the one hand and greater productivity and a better economic performance on the other, it is by no means crystal clear. Certainly, insofar as our more successful international trading competitors provide training programmes for their young people that are more modern and comprehensive than our own, then a *prima facie* case would seem to exist. However, their success would seem to depend in part on the establishment of structures of training which are coordinated and coherent and which involve a high degree of commitment from government, industry and business.

Given an uncertain future and the size and the number of the unknowns with which we are faced, we must devise a coherent and diversified pattern of provision for the 16-19 age group. This in turn requires us to break down the barriers between education and training and between the education service and industry. Most difficult of all, it requires us to overcome the meritocratic tradition by which we have distinguished, in order of prestige, between the 'educated', the 'trained' and the 'workers'. Traditionally, our system of secondary and further education has biased its provision to the disadvantage of the majority and to the detriment of technical and practical education [13]. One of the very few beneficial side effects of the tragic growth in youth unemployment has been to expose the considerable shortcomings in our provision of education and training for the 16-19 age group, shortcomings previously obscured by the tolerance and low demands for skill of too much youth unemployment. Paradoxically, we now have the opportunity to begin to remedy this state of affairs. If the opportunity is to be successfully grasped it will require the government to display the necessary leadership and the education and training service, industry, management and the trade unions to cooperate fully.

If, with some temerity, one were to suggest the broad outlines of a policy designed gradually to build up a coherent system of education and training for the 16-19 age group as a whole, they would be as follows. Firstly, we would introduce measures designed to increase our stock of competent technicians and craftsmen in those new industries and services resulting from technological developments, part of which would necessitate the reform and extension of our apprenticeship system to ensure that high standards of training are achieved. The quality of the training would be guaranteed by the state and, as in West Germany and Japan, employers would bear a significant part of the cost of training. The education service, industry and the government would work much more closely together to produce unified programmes of education and training. The current moves to introduce vocational elements into our secondary school curriculum would be strengthened and intensified. The Youth Training Scheme would be extended to two years, improvements in quality would be urgently sought, and its programmes would, where possible, be related to job opportunities. More young people, especially those from working class backgrounds, would be encouraged to stay on in full-time education after statutory school-leaving age by the systematic provision of education maintenance allowances. A wide-ranging programme of initial and in-service training would be instituted to provide sufficient numbers of well-qualified teachers to make these developments possible. The eventual overall aim of this policy would be to ensure that *all* young people in the 16-19 age group would in future receive some form of systematic education and/or training. Such a policy would not be inexpensive but, as a long term economic and social investment, it would be money well spent.

References

[1] Belbin, M., 'The YTS, a programme of early opportunity and long-term uncertainty', *BACIE Journal*, vol. 38, 1983, p. 139.

[2] Burghes, L. and Stagles, R., *No Choice at 16, a Study of Educational Maintenance Allowances*, Child Poverty Action Group, January 1983.

[3] Cantor, L.M. and Roberts, I.F., *Further Education Today, A Critical Review*, Second, Fully Revised Edition, Routledge and Kegan Paul, 1983, p. 52.

[4] Careers Service Advisory Council for England, 'Employment Problems of Young People from Ethnic Minorities', 1979.

[5] Department of Education and Science, *17+, A New Qualification*, May 1982.

[6] Department of Employment/Department of Education and Science, *Training for Jobs*, White Paper, *Cmnd* 9135, 1984.

[7] Hirsch, D., *Youth Unemployment: A Background Paper*, Youthaid, October 1983.

[8] Hollyhock, Bob, 'The college in its environment', *The Changing Face of Further Education*, FEU, December 1982, pp. 27–30.

[9] Manpower Services Commission, *A New Training Initiative: A Consultative Document*, May 1981, p. 9.

[10] Manpower Services Commission, *A New Training Initiative: An Agenda for Action*, December 1981.

[11] Prais, S.J., and Wagner, K., *Some Practical Aspects of Human Capital Investment: Training Standards in Five Occupations in Britain and Germany*, Discussion Paper no. 56, National Institute of Economic and Social Research, January 1983; and Schmidt, Hermann, 'The Federal Institute for Vocational Education', *BACIE Journal*, vol. 38, 1983.

[12] Raffe, D., 'The Transition from School to Work and the Recession: Evidence from the Scottish School Leavers Surveys, 1977–1983', Paper presented to the Standing Conference on the Sociology of Further Education, West Berlin, January 1984, pp. 10–11.

[13] Tomlinson, J., 'YTS and after: the implications for schools', *Secondary Education Journal*, vol. 13, no. 1, March 1983, pp. 14–15.

4   Skill Formation and Pay Relativities
by Ian S. Jones

Introduction

The provision of occupational skills for young people completing the period of compulsory schooling (which occurs at the age of 15 or 16 in most OECD countries) is undertaken either through workplace-based initial training schemes (such as apprenticeships) or in full-time vocational education. The two systems coexist, each tending to cater for a certain range of occupations (which varies from one country to another). France, the Benelux countries and Italy, for example, rely predominantly on full-time vocational education. In Britain and, amongst others, in Germany and Switzerland, apprenticeships or equivalent types of workplace-based initial training, often accompanied by part-time education, are more common than full-time education.

However, the incidence of apprenticeship training is also very much lower in Britain than in the other continental countries which rely on it as the primary means of intermediate skill formation. It may be argued that this difference reflects mainly so-called cultural factors, in particular the tendency for British apprenticeships to be confined to a relatively limited range of occupations (mainly associated with skilled manual and technician work in the manufacturing sector) and to be virtually non-existent in a wide range of clerical and junior administrative occupations and the retail trades. Cultural factors such as these are undoubtedly part of the story, but the incidence of apprenticeship is also significantly lower than in Germany and Switzerland even in those sectors of industry, notably engineering, where there is a strong apprenticeship tradition in Britain [14]. These current differences in the proportions of the labour force undergoing apprenticeship training are reflected in the higher proportion of the German and Swiss employees in engineering who are classified in national survey data either as engaged on skilled tasks (as opposed to semi- or unskilled work), or who have obtained certain qualifications which, in principle, would entitle them to do skilled work (table 4.1).

Although the number of young people entering apprenticeships is relatively low in Britain, it is clear from the evidence considered below that substantially more wished to do so at the going rates of apprentice pay. By contrast, in Germany, employers' demand for trainees has

Table 4.1   Distribution of the labour force by skill and qualification in engineering and related industries, per cent

	Britain	Germany	Switzerland
	1980	*1977*	
By skill [a]			
Skilled/craft	49.0 (37.8)	60.3	
Semi-skilled/operative	44.8 (48.7)	30.2	
Unskilled/other manual	6.2 (13.5)	9.6	
	1978	*1978*	*1979/80*
By qualification			
University	3.8	4.9	6.7
Intermediate	34.2	63.8	51.5
Low/none	62.0	31.3	41.8

Sources: Britain: *Department of Employment Gazette*, vol. 88, no. 10, October, 1980; Engineering Industry Training Board, *Annual Report and Accounts*, 1981/2; *National Institute Economic Review*, no. 98, November 1981: Germany: Saunders and Marsden, [16]; Switzerland: National Institute Discussion paper no. 54, 1982.

[a] Figures in parenthesis for Britain are the alternative definitions used by the EITB which probably conform more closely to the categories used in Germany.

tended to match the available supply. This chapter examines some of the possible causes and consequences of these outcomes.

The markets for trainees and for skilled labour
The issues involved may be clarified by an analysis of the markets for trainees and for skilled labour in a workplace-based training system. Outcomes in these two sectors of the labour market are closely related in such a context since the stock of skilled or trained workers available at any point of time largely reflects the past volume of trainee employment and also because the supply of trainees depends, *inter alia*, upon the expected earnings of skilled labour.

Assuming that the skills acquired in training are of a predominantly general or transferable nature and labour mobility relatively high, then firms' demand for trainees at any given wage depends very largely upon their productivity during the training period. At a given level of trainee productivity, the volume of trainee employment offered by firms will depend upon the costs incurred by the employer, including those involved in providing training. Trainee wage costs, including labour oncosts, are usually the major part of total cost [1] [4].

The supply of trainees depends upon the wages of trainees, of skilled adult labour and of non-skilled labour, which together determine the financial costs and benefits of acquiring skills. The supply of trainees at any given trainee wage is higher the higher is the expected return to training in the form of the differential between the wages of skilled and non-skilled labour.

Employers' demand for skilled labour at any given wage is a function of its productivity. In the short run, the supply of skilled labour is likely to be highly price inelastic. In the longer run, an increase (decrease) in the quantity of trainees employed by firms (and hence in the 'output' of skilled workers), will lead to an increase (decrease) in the supply of skilled workers.

If trainee pay increases as a result of minimum wage legislation, or trade union pressure, in the short run firms' demand for trainees declines. At the same time, the supply of potential trainees increases and there is an excess supply of trainees. If trainee wages are unresponsive to excess supply then, under competitive labour market conditions, the smaller output of skilled workers from training employment will in time lead to an increase in the differential between skilled and non-skilled. If institutional rigidities prevent such an outcome, however, then there will be a persistent excess demand for skilled labour.

This analysis suggests, therefore, that an examination of the pay differentials between trainees and other workers on the one hand, and between skilled and non-skilled workers on the other, may throw some light on the labour market outcomes noted earlier.

Pay differentials
The relationship between trainee and adult pay in Britain, Germany and Switzerland

A possible complicating factor in international comparisons of trainee pay is that the duration of apprenticeships may vary from one country to another. Since the 1960s, when many apprenticeships were of five years' or even longer duration, the average length of apprenticeship in Britain has fallen steadily and now stands at about three to four years. This is closely comparable to practice in both Switzerland (where most apprenticeships are also of three to four years' duration) and Germany where the normal term is from three to three and half years. In all three countries the longer apprenticeships tend to be in engineering craft and electrical occupations.

Table 4.2 sets out the basic rates of trainee pay as a proportion of the basic pay of craft or skilled workers in corresponding British and German collective pay agreements. In Switzerland, trainee pay is excluded from collective bargaining; it is determined by individual employers and there are quite wide variations even within particular occupations.

Table 4.2   Basic or standard trainee pay as a proportion of the basic pay of adult
skilled workers in certain British (1981) and German (1979)
collective agreements

	Chemicals	Engineering metals [a]	Building/construction [b]	Motor mechanic	Textiles	Clothing	Electrical
Britain by age							
16	56	47	43	43	50	67	40
17	65	60	70	50	63	79	45
18	82	75	90	65	75	88	50
19	88	90	—	85	90	92	65
20	95	100	—	100	—	—	80
Average	*78*	*75*	*68*	*68*	*72*	*83*	*55*
Germany by year							
1	31	29	24	21	32	30	17
2	36	32	37	22	37	33	21
3	41	35	47	25	42	38	24
4	46	40	—	—	46	—	28
Average	*37*	*33*	*36*	*23*	*38*	*34*	*22*

Sources: Britain: Department of Employment, *Times Rates and Hours of Pay*; April 1981:
Germany: Münich, J. and Jung, E., [12], Noll, I., Beicht, U., Wiederhold-Fritz, S.,
[13], Williams, S. *et al* [20].
[a] Engineering in Britain, metalworking industries in Germany.
[b] By year of apprentieship in Britain.

One difference to emerge is that whereas the rates of minimum trainee pay were (and still are) mainly specified acccording to the age of the trainee in most British collective agreements, in Germany trainees are paid according to the year of training. For purposes of comparison, it is assumed that the representative British trainee enters the apprenticeship at age 16½ and completes three and a half to four years' training at age 20 or 20½. On this assumption, it can be seen that, on average, a British apprentice paid the minimum rate specified in the agreement, would have received some 50 per cent of the minimum rate of a skilled worker even in his first year of apprenticeship, which, in many cases, is now spent entirely in off-the-job training. His German counterpart, who would probably spend a somewhat higher proportion of his time in productive work, would have received about 20–30 per cent of the minimum adult skilled rate. In the fourth training year, the British apprentice would receive about 95 per cent of the adult minimum rate, compared to about 30–45 per cent in Germany. Thus, with the exception of the trainee building craftsman in Germany, whose pay roughly doubles between the first and third year of apprenticeship, German trainees receive a more modest rate of pay increase than British trainees over the term of their training and moreover start from a very much lower base (as a proportion of the minimum adult skilled rate). Over the term of the apprenticeship, a British apprentice paid the minimum rate specified in the collective agreement would receive about three-quarters of the minimum skilled rate compared to perhaps 30–35 per cent in Germany.

Data from the 1974 New Earnings Survey (NES) indicate that the hourly earnings of male apprentices were then some 53 per cent of those of all adult male manual workers – a significantly smaller proportion than that of apprentices' basic pay to the basic pay of skilled manual workers over the apprenticeship period. This is because adults worked longer hours than apprentices and also received proportionately more supplementary payments. By contrast, in both Germany (in 1981) and Switzerland (in 1979) the hourly earnings of male trainees were only about a fifth of those of adult male manual workers [7]. Thus the hourly earnings of British apprentices in 1974 were some 2½ times higher as a proportion of adult male manual workers' earnings than those of Swiss and German trainees in 1979 and 1981 respectively, a very similar relationship to that observed earlier between the basic wage rates of apprentices and skilled adult workers in Britain and Germany.

The following scattered pieces of evidence suggest that there does not seem to have been any significant recent change in the British relativities. First, there has been little change in the structure of minimum rates of pay negotiated for apprentices in national collective agreements since 1974. If anything, there has been some tendency for apprentices' minimum pay to drift upwards as a proportion of the minimum adult skilled rate, for example, in the engineering agreement [7]. Second, data on the hourly wage costs of apprentices and other full-time trainees has been collected in the EC Labour Cost Surveys for 1979 and 1981. Estimates obtained from the 1981 survey indicate that in Index of Production (IOP) industries, the ratio of the hourly wage costs (excluding labour oncosts) of manual trainees to those of adult male manual workers was very similar to the 53 per cent relativity observed in the 1974 NES data [7]. Finally, from the NES, there appears to have been little change in the pay of all male manual workers under the age of 21 as a proportion of the pay of adult male manual workers since 1974 [7].

According to the 1983 NES, the average weekly earnings of adult male manual workers in April 1983 (excluding those whose pay was affected by absence) were some £152.2 in all IOP industries and £147.7 in manufacturing industries. If the earnings relativities between apprentices and adult male workers in Britain had been the same as those observed in Germany and Switzerland, then British apprentices in April 1983 might have received on average about £30 a week over the term of their apprenticeship. This figure may be compared with the actual basic pay of apprentices in the agreements shown in table 4.2, which increased from about £40 a week in the first year of apprenticeship to about £80 in the fourth year, and with the £25 a week basic trainee allowance recommended for YTS participants.

The pay of apprentices and of other young persons in employment
Table 4.3 shows the basic pay (or allowance) of trainees and of other young workers negotiated in the British and German collective agreements referred to in table 4.2 above. We see that the relative pay of trainees in the British agreements is radically different from that observed in the German agreements. Whereas the basic pay of British apprentices is some 10–20 per cent higher than that of non-apprentices of the same age, in Germany the basic trainee allowances are only 40–45 per cent of the basic pay of other young workers – with the exception of building trades apprentices where the relativity is about 60 per cent.

Table 4.3   *Average basic pay of trainee and non-trainee in British (1981) and German (1979) collective agreements*

	Chemicals	Engineering metals [a]	Construc- tion	Motor mechanic	Textiles	Clothing
Britain £ per week						
1. Apprentice	68.00	58.95	54.50	48.78	—	—
2. Non-apprentice	52.59	45.44	50.32	42.75	—	—
1 as per cent of 2	*129*	*130*	*108*	*114*	—	—
Germany DM per month						
1. Trainee	582	511	800	—	470	436
2. Non-trainee	1360	1200	1350	—	1040	1041
1 as per cent of 2	*43*	*43*	*59*	—	*45*	*42*

Sources: As table 4.2.
[a] Engineering in Britain, metalworking industries in Germany.

The actual earnings of apprentices are likely to be a smaller proportion of those of non-apprentices of the same age than those shown in table 4.3, because young employees doing unskilled or semi-skilled work are more likely than apprentices to have their basic pay supplemented by bonuses and overtime payments [7]. Consequently, a somewhat different picture emerges from an analysis of relative earnings using the 1974 NES data. These suggest that the average weekly earnings of apprentices then were only some 70 per cent of those of non-apprenticed male manual workers under the age of 21. However, the figure of 70 per cent almost certainly exaggerates the true wage-for-age differential. The average age of the apprentice population in the 1974 NES was less than the average age of non-apprentice manual workers aged 20 or less [7] and there is a strong wage-for-age relationship amongst workers in this age group.

In Switzerland, official earnings survey data for 1979 indicates that the hourly earnings of male apprentices in both manual and non-manual occupations were only about 30 per cent of those of young men in unskilled and semi-skilled occupations. Hourly earnings of female trainees were some 40 per cent of those of non-trainee young women in the 15–19 age group [7].

Even if British apprentices earned only 70 per cent of the earnings of non-apprentices of the same age over their apprenticeship, it would mean that they would have made only a relatively modest sacrifice in terms of current income foregone in acquiring craft or technician status by comparison with German and Swiss trainees. Yet, the subsequent monetary premia for the acquisition of skills appear at first sight to be very similar in the three countries, as we shall see.

The relationship between the pay of adults and of non-trainee young people
Implicit in the results presented so far on the relationships between the pay of trainees and adults on the one hand, and between trainees and non-trainee young people on the other, is the differential between the pay of adults and those of non-trainee young people.

For Britain, the 1974 NES data indicate that, on average, the weekly earnings of non-apprentice male manual workers aged less than 21 were then some 69 per cent of those of all adult male manual workers. The Swiss earnings survey data for 1979 show that the hourly earnings of non-trainee male workers aged 19 or less were some 66 per cent of those of unskilled and semi-skilled adult male manual workers and some 57 per cent of those of skilled adult male manual workers. Given the difference in age composition between the young workers group in Britain on the one hand and the two continental countries on the other and the strong wage-for-age relationship in Britain, the relativities observed in the three countries appear to be very similar.

Adult skill differentials
About 85 per cent of the male apprentices in the 1974 NES sample were employed in manual occupations (almost half of the remainder being technicians). Attention may therefore be focussed on the pay differential enjoyed by skilled manual workers as an indicator of the monetary rewards associated with the acquisition of skilled status through apprenticeship or equivalent training. Perhaps a quarter of all British apprentices are employed in the 1968 SIC Orders VII (mechanical engineering), IX (electrical engineering), XI (vehicles) and XII (metal goods n.e.s.). Table 4.4 shows the estimated earnings of skilled manual workers relative to those of all other manual workers in

these industries in 1980 and compares these relativities with those enjoyed by skilled manual workers in Germany and Switzerland.

Table 4.4   Skilled male manual workers' gross earnings as a proportion of the earnings of all other manual workers in Britain, Germany and Switzerland

Britain (1980)		Germany (1980)				Switzerland (1979)
Engineering		Engineering		Industry [a]		All manual occupations
Hourly	weekly	Hourly	weekly	Hourly	weekly	Hourly
114.5	117.5	114.4	115.4	113.8	114.3	116.3

Sources: Britain: *Department of Employment Gazette*, vol. 88, no. 10, October, 1980; Germany: *Statistisches Bundesamt* [18]; Switzerland: unpublished tabulations provided by Dr H. Hollenstein, E.T.H., Zurich.

[a] Corresponds roughly to British Index of Production industries.

The differentials between the pay of skilled and other manual workers shown in table 4.4 are remarkably similar in the three countries, especially in view of the very different pay bargaining structures in operation and also in view of the differences in the proportions of each type of worker in the labour force (see tables 4.1 and 4.2 above). Given their relative abundance in Germany and Switzerland, it might have been expected that skilled workers would have commanded a somewhat smaller differential over their unskilled colleagues than in Britain.

By comparison with the British differentials, those for Germany and Switzerland may slightly exaggerate the returns to apprentice training. This is because, in the British survey data, the 'skilled worker' category is defined in terms of workers who have completed an apprenticeship or received equivalent training. Whilst most German and Swiss skilled workers are also likely to be apprentice-trained, there might also be a proportion of apprentice-trained workers in the semi-skilled group in the two countries.

With this qualification and bearing in mind too that the British figures are directly relevant only to perhaps a quarter of the apprentice stock, the figures in table 4.4 are taken to indicate that, when expressed as a proportion of the earnings available in non-skilled occupations, the monetary reward available to those undertaking whatever initial training is necessary for entry to skilled manual occupations is unlikely to differ radically between the three countries.

The supply of and demand for trainees

Under competitive labour market conditions trainee wages would tend towards the level at which supply and demand are in balance with each other. An excess supply of trainees would put downward pressure on wages and an excess demand would have the opposite effect. An examination of the available evidence suggests that whereas in Britain there has been a persistent excess supply of trainees, in Germany there has been an approximate balance in recent years between the numbers of training places offered by employers and of those seeking apprenticeships, as shown in table 4.5.

Table 4.5   Estimates of the supply of and demand for trainees in Germany, 1974-81, training places, thousands

Year	Places offered by employers	Applicants	Unfilled [a] places	Unplaced applicants [a]
1974	479.4	470.4	29.4	20.7
1975	481.3	485.5	19.3	23.5
1976	517.7	526.5	18.9	27.7
1977	585.3	585.4	26.9	27.0
1978	621.6	623.2	22.3	23.8
1979	677.2	660.0	36.9	19.7
1980	694.6	667.4	44.6	17.3
1981	642.7	627.5	37.3	22.1

Sources: Bundesminister für Bildung und Wissenschaft [2], Berufliche Bildung, table 3.
[a] As notified to local employment offices.

We see that in four out of the eight years between 1974 and 1981 there has been a small gross surplus of training places. The data on unoccupied training places and unplaced applicants indicates that the extent of local labour market imbalances within the overall balance for the economy as a whole was probably very modest.

It should also be noticed that a continuing balance between supply and demand has been achieved despite an increase of about 40 per cent in the number of applicants for training places between 1974/5 and 1979/80 and the onset of recession in 1980/1, without any need on the part of the Federal authorities to subsidise the provision of training places by private employers. Between 1976 and 1980 the German federal government in fact had reserve powers to levy all employers with more than 25 employees and to use the proceeds to fund additional training places if the forecast demand for trainees in Germany as a whole did not exceed the expected supply of trainees by at least 12.5 per cent. The levy power was never invoked and lapsed completely in 1980 following a ruling in the constitutional court that the federal government had no competence to intervene in the finance of vocational training. However, it has been suggested that the existence of these reserve powers may well have encouraged the provision of additional training places by employers whose representative organisations were strongly opposed to the legislation in the first place [15].

In contrast, several studies have concluded that there has been a persistent excess in the number of young people seeking apprenticeships compared to the volume of apprentice recruitment by employers in Britain since at least the mid-1950s [11]. In the 1970s, this has occurred despite the existence of financial incentives to companies to employ additional apprentices offered by some of the Training Boards established under the 1964 Training Act.

Employers themselves, especially larger firms, have consistently reported an excess of applicants for apprentice places over the number of places on offer, even during periods such as the 1950s or 1960s when there was probably excess demand for young workers as a whole [6]. Although fears have been expressed from time to time that the steadily increasing proportion of young people staying on at school beyond the minimum school-leaving age may be reducing the supply of more highly qualified candidates for apprenticeships [6], there is so far very little evidence that firms have been unable to recruit the required numbers of suitably qualified apprentices.

A recent EITB report [17] sheds interesting light on the supply of and demand for apprentices in the engineering sector. Since the early 1970s, the Board has taken the view that recruitment of first-year craft and technician apprentices by firms in the engineering industry has been insufficient to meet the long-term demands of the industry for skilled personnel. The Board therefore directly recruits young people for first-year apprentice training under its training award or extra recruitment schemes. These trainees receive a training allowance worth about two-thirds the basic rate for first-year apprentices under the engineering industry agreement. In 1977 there were nearly 11,000 applicants for some 2,900 training places under the scheme. To put these figures in perspective, firms in scope to the EITB recruited less than 22,000 for first-year craft and technician training in the same year [5].

Statistical analyses by Lindley [8] [9] have found that variations in the volume of apprentice recruitment into the engineering industry in the period 1951-71 were much better explained by factors reflecting the varying conditions of employers' demand than variation in the potential supply of trainees. In particular, Lindley found that whilst the volume of recruitment of young people into unskilled and semi-skilled employment in the engineering industry was highly correlated with variations in the number of 15 and 16 year old school-leavers (a labour supply factor), apprentice recruitment was not significantly related to underlying demographic changes. A statistically significant relationship between apprentice recruitment into the engineering industry and the total number of young workers is also absent in the period since 1966/7; specifically, the correlation between year-to-year changes in the volume of apprentice recruitment and the number of workers aged 18 and less is 0.08 for the period 1966/7–1981/2. A later study by Merrilees [11], has also explained a high proportion of the variation in recruitment of first-year apprentices into the engineering industry in the period 1963–79 by demand-side factors.

The significance of these statistical results can best be appreciated with the aid of a supply and demand diagram. In chart 4.1, WT_0 is the apprentice wage which would balance supply and demand for trainees. However, suppose, as appears to have been the case in Britain, that the going rate for apprentices is highly insensitive to supply and demand pressures and changes only slowly over time. Wages might then be set at WT_1 (where there would be an excess supply of trainees) or WT_2 (where there would be excess demand) and in neither case would there be a strong tendency for wages to adjust to WT_0.

Chart 4.1   The demand for and supply of trainees

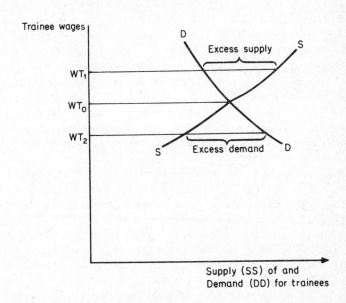

Given a wage WT_1, changes in the volume of apprentice employment would tend to be highly correlated with factors causing shifts in the firms' demand for labour; conversely, assuming that variations in the labour supply function were relatively uncorrelated with variations in demand, then they would tend not to be closely related to changes in apprentice intake. On the other hand, if wages were set at WT_2, with excess demand from firms, then variations in apprentice intake would tend to be closely correlated with factors causing changes in the supply of trainees. Given a highly inflexible wages structure, the finding that variations in apprentice intake are well explained by demand-side factors, but are largely unexplained by labour supply-side influences, may therefore be taken as further evidence that the market has been characterised by an excess supply of trainees.

Trainee pay and employers' demand for trainees
The statistical studies by Lindley [9] and Merrilees [11] suggest that a reduction of 10 per cent in the relativity between the pay of apprentices and adult workers would have increased employers' demand for apprentices in the British engineering industry approximately proportionately in the 1960s and 1970s, all other things being equal.

Also relevant here is the limited evidence so far available on the responses of firms and of young people to the Government's YTS initiative. Under the scheme, 16 year old school-leavers and unemployed 17 year olds are guaranteed a 12-month programme combining further education and work experience. They are treated as trainees (rather than as employees) and receive a trainee allowance, the recommended value of which (£25 a week) is considerably less than the going rate received by apprentices and other young employees. In order to participate, firms must satisfy certain criteria laid down by the MSC regarding the number of recruits and the quality of training offered. Firms participating in the scheme then receive a grant worth approximately £2,000 for each 16 year old recruited, including young people recruited as employees rather than as YTS trainees, intended to cover the cost of the training allowance and of training provision. In effect, therefore, the YTS produces a very substantial reduction in the supply price of trainees to firms both through the reduction in trainee pay and through the payment of an employment subsidy. These incentives have been sufficient to ensure that the number of training places available under YTS has comfortably exceeded the number of young people seeking places on the scheme [3].

Public policy implications
In summary, assuming that the technical conditions of production and hence the relative productivity of skilled, non-skilled and trainee labour at given factor proportions are similar, the structure of pay differentials which has evolved in the British system of collective

bargaining is seriously at odds with the requirements of a workplace-based initial training system. Compared with the situation in Germany and Switzerland, the relatively high trainee pay in Britain deters employers from offering apprenticeships. At the same time, young people are encouraged to apply for apprenticeships given the financial rewards available to skilled workers and the relatively small or even non-existent financial sacrifices involved in skilled training. The outcome may be described as one of market failure, the nature of which lies not so much on the demand side (as some recent analyses of British training problems have suggested [10]) but rather in the failure of trainee pay to fall to its market clearing level in the face of persistent excess supply.

The level of trainee pay in Britain is largely determined by voluntary collective agreements between employers and trade unions and may therefore be taken to reflect the perceptions of the parties involved as to what is an appropriate level. Such perceptions may be shaped by deeply-held social attitudes, for example, about the worth of trainees compared to other young workers. In these circumstances, a public policy designed to secure a higher volume of apprentice training, closer to that currently achieved in Germany and Switzerland, and to what might occur in the absence of wage rigidities, will almost certainly require some element of payroll subsidy to reduce the costs of employing trainees and hence to increase employers' demand for them. The scale of subsidy could be limited, however, if eligibility was restricted to firms paying trainees an allowance considerably less than the current rates of apprentice pay. Initial payment of the subsidy might also be linked to the conclusion of a training contract guaranteeing the trainees' rights to further education and, in time, to supervision by suitably qualified training personnel equivalent to the German *Meister*. Continuing support over the term of the training programme should be linked to the trainees' success in externally-examined tests of proficiency. A trainee payroll subsidy scheme could therefore be used as an instrument to affect both the quantity and quality of intermediate skill training.

In very broad strategic terms such a scheme may be contrasted with the current YTS in the following way. YTS effectively segregates the population of 16 year old school-leavers into a relatively small group of those entering apprenticeships (currently numbering only 15 per cent of the 16 year old school-leaving population) and the large majority entering employment with a very limited training content or the YTS. YTS trainees are offered a relatively thin spread (one year) of training and work experience. As such, the scheme has been rightly criticised as an unsatisfactory compromise between training and social policy objectives [19]. The alternative approach would aim at a major expansion in the number of people undertaking extended initial training courses. It should be remembered that in Germany and Switzerland, apprenticeship programmes of at least two and very often of three to four years' duration are undertaken by three-quarters or more of the 15–18 year old age group not engaged in full-time education.

Any serious reform of initial training arrangements along these lines would probably require major complementary changes in the British secondary school curriculum. As noted earlier, given the relatively small demand for apprentices, firms do not appear to have any difficulty in recruiting apprentices with whatever minimum educational qualifications are considered necessary. However, a substantial expansion of demand from employers could be frustrated by an insufficient supply of young people with the general educational attainments necessary to benefit from apprenticeship or equivalent types of extended initial training programmes.

References

[1] Atkinson, J., *Evaluation of Apprentice Support Awards*, Institute of Manpower Studies, 1982.
[2] Bundesminister für Bildung und Wissenschaft, *Grund-und-Struktur Daten, 1982/83*, Munich, Gersbach und Sohn Verlag, 1982.
[3] Department of Employment, 'Employment Topics', *Employment Gazette*, Volume 92, No. 2, February 1984.
[4] Edding, F., *et al*, *Kosten und Finanzierung der ausserschulischen beruflichen Bildung, Abschlussbericht der Sachverständigenkommission Kosten und Finanzierung der beruflichen Bildung*, Bielefeld, Bertelsmann Verlag, 1974.
[5] Engineering Industry Training Board, *Annual Report and Accounts, 1981/2*, Watford, EITB, 1982.
[6] Fogarty, M.P., Reid, E., *Differentials for Managers and Skilled Manual Workers*, Policy Studies Institute, Report No. 586, London, PSI, 1980.
[7] Jones, I.S., *The costs and benefits of skill acquisition*, National Institute discussion paper, forthcoming.
[8] Lindley, R.M. 'Manpower movements and the supply of labour', in *Problems in Manpower Forecasting*, Wabe, J. (ed), Farnborough, Saxon House, 1974.
[9] Lindley, R.M., 'The demand for apprentice recruits by the engineering industry 1951–71', *Scottish Journal of Political Economy*, February 1975.
[10] Manpower Services Commission, *The New Training Initiative: an Agenda for Action*, London, MSC, 1981.
[11] Merrilees, W.J., 'Alternative models of apprentice recruitment with special reference to the British engineering industry', *Applied Economics*, February 1983.
[12] Münch, J. and Jung, E., 'Jugendarbeitslosigkeit und Berufsbildung: Sozialer und materieller Status von Jugendlichen beim Übergang von der Schule zum Beruf in der Bundesrepublik Deutschland', Berlin, CEDEFOP, 1980.

[13] Noll, I., Beicht, U., Wiederhold–Fritz, S., *Ausbildungsvergütungen nach Ausbildungsberufen*, Berlin, Bundesinstitut für Berufsbildung, 1980.

[14] Prais, S.J. and Wagner, K., 'Some practical aspects of human capital investment: training standards in five occupations in Britain and Germany', *National Institute Economic Review*, No. 105, August 1983.

[15] Reardon, R., 'Supply and demand put pressure on West Germany's youth training', *Employment Gazette*, Volume 91, no. 1, January, 1983.

[16] Saunders, C.T. and Marsden, D., *Pay Inequalities in the European Communities*, London, Butterworth, 1980.

[17] Sinclair, E., *Selection of Craft and Technician Trainees*, EITB Reference Paper 2/82, Watford, EITB, 1982.

[18] Statistisches Bundesamt, *Löhne und Gehälter*, Fachserie 16, Reihe 2.1, Arbeiterverdienste in der Industrie, January 1980.

[19] Wellens, J., 'Comment on the Youth Training Scheme', *Industrial and Commercial Training*, Volume 14, no. 6, June 1982.

[20] Williams, S. *et al*, *Youth Without Work*, Paris, OECD, 1981.

5 What can we learn from the German System of Education and Vocational Training?
by S. J. Prais

Background

For over a century careful observers, including the great Cambridge economist Alfred Marshall, have warned that the educational sytem of this country was not well adapted to the needs of modern scientifically based industry. Britain's industrial leadership would be overtaken not only by the United States – with its great natural resources and its enterprising immigrant population – but also by Germany, with its highly developed educational and vocational training system, as by other European countries on the same path. Two disastrous world wars intervened; and it was not until the 1960s that productivity in German manufacturing industry eventually overtook that in Britain. By 1980, output per employee in manufacturing was some 50 per cent higher in Germany than in Britain and real income per head of the total population was about a third higher. Much of the rest of European industry seems now more or less at the same productivity level as Germany's and well ahead of Britain [7]. Unemployment has risen in Germany since 1980 but, partly because of the emigration of *Gastarbeiter*, it has not risen to the same extent as here (8 per cent of the total German labour force, compared to 12 per cent in Britain unemployed at the end of 1983 [2]); the more worrying difference is in youth unemployment: of all 16–25 year olds, 15 per cent were unemployed in Germany in early 1983, compared with 28 per cent in Britain. It seems more than probable that vocational training arrangements in the two countries have contributed to that difference [3].

Differences in productivity are obviously not solely determined by differences in education and training. Economists usually look to factors such as plant sizes, extent of specialisation in production, degree of competitiveness, usage of machinery, supply of capital funds to new firms, and the amiability of labour relations. However, a comparison of ten major industries between Britain and Germany, carried out at the National Institute and published at the end of 1981, came to the conclusion that, from the point of view of productivity, there were particularly important differences between these countries in two factors: labour relations, as manifested by the incidence of strikes, especially in large plants, and the extent of vocationally qualified manpower [8].

This latter factor is the concern of the present paper; it summarises the National Institute's more recent and detailed comparisons of vocational training and associated aspects of schooling in Britain and Germany [9, 10, 11]. It concentrates on a limited number of aspects bearing on economic performance and, more particularly, on those where policy in Britain might benefit from German experience. This is not to suggest that Germany may not have much to learn from certain parts of Britain's educational system; but that is not the subject of this chapter. It also needs saying at the outset – since efficiency is not always compatible with variety – that there is considerably less regional and local variation in the German educational system than in ours, but we shall not deal with that question here.

Vocational training

The contrasts between the two countries in the scope of vocational training may serve as our starting point though, as we shall see, the foundations for those contrasts are already well laid at the schooling stage. Broadly speaking, in Germany attendance at part-time vocational courses is compulsory after the end of compulsory full-time schooling till the age of 18 – that is usually for three years – for all not continuing in full-time education. Anyone in that age group may be employed only at approved establishments, where he or she follows a training course in the chosen occupation (*Beruf*, literally 'calling') under the supervision of a master craftsman or someone of similar qualification. One day each week the trainee attends a vocational school (*Berufschule*), where just over half the time is devoted to vocational studies and the remainder to general subjects. We need not concern ourselves here with the special provisions that apply to the minority who are unemployed and to those embarking on unskilled work; the important point is that the great majority of those who leave school at the minimum leaving age continue combined courses of training and vocational education for about three years. Examinations are taken at intermediate and final stages leading ultimately to qualification as a recognised craftsman.

While compulsory *full*-time schooling ends in Germany generally at 15, taken together with these *part*-time courses there is a sense in which education is compulsory till 18. The part-time element in the German system at the older ages is not necessarily a disadvantage on balance, since many pupils find they make 'better sense' of their school studies when placed in the context of practical applications.

This kind of training combined with part-time schooling is also familiar in Britain and is similar to that undertaken, for example, by an apprenticed electrician. But it needs to be asked whether the qualifications reached in the two countries can really be of the same standard if courses of this type are taken, not by the small and select proportion of the age group who take apprenticeships in Britain, but by the much greater proportion obliged to take them in Germany. The answer seems to be Yes, on the basis of comparisons we made between the two countries of five relatively popular training courses: electrician, mechanical fitter, construction worker, office clerk, and employees in retailing. The comparisons were based on an exchange of examination papers between instructors or examiners in the two countries who were able to identify similar levels of qualification. The syllabuses were of course not identical: sometimes a course in one country was found to be broader in scope than in the other and this usually went with less specialised depth; but, on the whole, there was a fair correspondence between the two countries in what was taught in three years on a day-release basis.

Nevertheless, there are two general differences that deserve mention here. First, *practical tests* which form an essential part of the German qualification system have been unusual in this country in the past two decades. These tests in Germany are often detailed and extensive and are carried out under examination conditions. The building trades provide an example where practical tests in the final examination may extend over two days. For mechanical fitters or toolmakers a day's test is not unusual. A shop assistant's practical test may last only an hour with oral questions, for example, on the quality of the materials and maintenance procedures of specimen goods which the examiner is 'buying', and with the candidate going through the full 'sales routine', right up to suggestions of related items that the customer may need. In order to qualify at the final examination it is necesary to pass both in theoretical written papers and in the practical test. Qualifications in Germany are thus less likely to be regarded as 'mere paper qualifications' a dismissive attitude often found in England.

The building industry in England is exceptional in that, because of declining standards of craftsmanship, it has decided to reintroduce in 1985 practical testing for its apprentices which had been abolished in the mid-1970s as part of a general move towards 'in-course assessment'. German training establishments were visited by the Construction Industry Training Board to benefit from current practice there. Perhaps other trades should follow the same path. The reputation of our manufactures is no longer what it was some decades ago, when the 'Made in England' mark was synonymous with quality of the highest international standards. There is now a widely-felt need to raise standards of craftsmanship. One can only wonder whether moves towards the introduction (or reintroduction) of practical testing of craft skills should not be vigorously encouraged by the government, making any training subsidies dependent on a suitably phased programme.

A second general difference between the countries could be detected in those aspects of vocational courses that required mathematical reasoning, or even just basic arithmetical processes; here German standards seemed to be higher. German vocational examinations usually include a separate question paper on applied mathematics relevant to the particular occupation. In England, mathematical aspects are not examined separately, but are implicitly tested in the relevant subject papers; the net effect seems to be that mathematics is given less emphasis. The difference in mathematical standards appeared in both technical and administrative occupations. It was particularly clear in electricians' examinations, especially where complex circuitry was involved; but it was also apparent in relation to office training, where all German trainees are obliged to take courses both in secretarial work, such as audio-typing and commercial correspondence, and also in book-keeping – while in England courses in book-keeping are unpopular and are infrequently taken by clerical trainees. Wider instruction in book-keeping presents problems in England stemming, so it appears, from low school attainments in arithmetic. Complaints about Britain's productive efficiency have centred as much on delays in delivery, poor stock control, poor progress chasing and so on, as on the technical quality of the goods [6]. It is thus important not to underestimate the importance of raising the standards of those concerned with administrative and clerical functions. Here again there is scope for policy intervention (by attaching conditions to training subsidies) designed to increase mathematical competence during vocational training; but much obviously needs to be done to lay better mathematical foundations at school.

Just over half of the relevant age group in Germany in 1980 embarked on such combined work training and part-time vocational courses. Not all trainees complete their course as qualified craftsmen; some fail, some leave before their final examination, and others climb onto the various ladders that lead to higher qualifications. The important contrast with Britain is that for many decades there have been well laid out career paths involving graded courses, examinations and recognised qualifications – for that broad middle section of the population which lies between, on the one hand, those who go on to university or otherwise enter a profession and, on the other hand, those who are unskilled. This contrast shows itself very clearly in sample population surveys which include questions on vocational qualifications (the *Mikrozensus* in Germany, the General Household Survey in Britain). The German survey for 1978 recorded two-thirds of the German labour force as having a vocational or higher qualification (that is to say, had passed examinations at the craftsman level, based on their day-release courses, or above). Only a third of the German workforce were without vocational qualifications. The British surveys for 1974–8 showed almost precisely the reverse proportions: some two-thirds were vocationally unqualified and only a third – at the most – could be regarded as having intermediate vocational or higher qualifications including those who had simply served their time. The difference lay only marginally in the proportions with university qualifications (5.5 per cent in Britain, 7.1 per cent in Germany). Virtually all the difference lay in the sector with intermediate qualifications. Per head of the workforce, at least twice as many qualify each year in Germany as mechanics, electricians and construction workers as in Britain; the multiple is very much higher in broadly-qualified office workers and in distribution [10].

There is scope for debate as to whether such an extended and broad system of vocational training as Germany's is necessary and to what extent it can be justified on economic grounds. The training of shop assistants provides an example: before the rise of self-service stores, training in stock records and basic book-keeping would not have come amiss in a competent shop assistant, but German retailing employers now question whether a full three years' course, covering these and wider aspects of customer service, is still necessary for the typical range of duties of an assistant in a modern supermarket. Would not two years be enough for such an occupation? Or perhaps even one year (as in Switzerland in this occupation, though in other respects that country's training system is close to Germany's) [4]. Similar questions are debated in other occupations. It is worth remarking that German labour unions seem to be very much on the side of longer three year courses for everyone, even though it means that young persons remain for longer on low trainee allowances. The desire to reduce invidious distinctions amongst different classes of trainees may be uppermost in their minds, but there is also the desire to provide everyone, even those embarking on less skilled occupations, with a broader competence and a degree of potential flexibility which becomes possible on a longer course.

The issue of 'how much training' is complex, because technical advance in the past has often done as much to 'de-skill' many production jobs, as to require more advanced skills in the making, maintenance and setting up of new machinery [12]. The early success of American industry, as subsequently of modern industry elsewhere, lay precisely in that Tayloristic sub-division of labour and de-skilling of jobs which enabled the unskilled immigrant to master rapidly a very limited task, to be carried out proficiently with the help of relatively simple machines and jigs. In the present generation automation has gone further still, for it is now concerned with transferring to machines of great complexity the assembly and routine mechanical tasks carried out by the unskilled operator of yesterday's machines. Industrial success in earlier decades in Britain managed well enough by combining a few highly skilled engineers with a large and basically unskilled workforce; the provision of broad-scale systematic training for the latter may well have been unjustifiable then on any calculation of immediate economic returns. With the progressive elimination of unskilled labur by automated and robotised machines on the factory floor, and by computers and word-processors in offices, the demand for those of technician calibre has become even greater and the industrial success of countries accustomed to a high standard of living now depends on a labour force in which the average person is skilled. Technically advanced industries sometimes still find work for an unskilled labour force, but unskilled operations carried out on a large scale tend to be transferred to countries where wages are low (south-east Asia); if high real wages continue to be demanded on behalf of a largely unskilled labour force, unemployment is likely to result.

Germany's system of upgrading the general level of skills of its labour force may well have been adopted in advance of its immediate necessities; looked at today, in the light of current technological trends and their impact on the demand for unskilled labour, its well-developed and successful system provides an example worthy of detailed study and wider emulation. We need to know more of their methods of 'practical education' and how training requirements are being adapted to current technological developments. Such comparisons are not easy, and our institutional research framework for such purposes is still slender; there would be great benefits from strengthening it.

Schooling
The standards reached by vocational trainees in Germany and the broad sector of the population that attains them, are very much dependent on school-leaving attainments. If Britain wished to match German vocational training, it would be necessary first to attend to what it is that our *typical* schools *actually* achieve – not merely what our *best* schools *attempt* to achieve – both in general schooling and in vocationally-related subjects.

As will be familiar, comparisons of schooling attainments are far from straightforward, not least because of difference in organisation. The German schooling system is based mainly on selection, having regard to ability at ages 10–12; only 3 per cent of their secondary pupils are in comprehensive schools, compared with our 90 per cent.

The three principal types of school in Germany are, first, Main schools, which correspond broadly to our previous Secondary Modern schools; secondly, Intermediate schools, which correspond in some ways to our earlier Technical and Central schools, but with a broader curriculum and catering for a much larger proportion of the age group; and, thirdly, Grammar schools. (The German terms are *Hauptschulen*, *Realschulen* and *Gymnasien*: it will be convenient here to refer to them as Main, Intermediate and Grammar schools; the small percentage in private schools in the two countries may be ignored here). There are opportunities for moving from one type of school to another at the end of each school year, depending on attainments. About a fifth of all German school-leavers come from grammar schools, which is not very different from previous practice in this country; the remainder are divided at present more or less equally between the other two school types. The Intermediate type has expanded most rapidly in recent decades, with a tripling in numbers of pupils in the past twenty years; this type is expected to overtake the Main school, which had previously been numerically the largest, by the mid-1980s.

A school-leaving certificate appropriate to each type of school is usually awarded on the basis of final-year tests, both written and oral, together with in-course assessments. The award is based on average attainments in a broad curriculum of some ten subjects, subject to the important proviso on minimum attainments in core subjects – usually mathematics, science, native language and sometimes a foreign language. The precise curriculum requirements and methods of assessment vary according to *Land* and type of school, subject to a broad Federal agreement for equivalence of standards. It is perhaps worth noting here that a foreign language (usually English) is an obligatory part of the curriculum even in their Main schools which cater for the lowest ability range. Class repeating is a common practice for pupils not reaching the required standard at the end of each year in second schools and may help to maintain pupils' incentives. It also considerably reduces the dispersion of attainments: the coefficient of variation of mathematical attainments of 13–14 year olds in English Secondary Modern schools was nearly double that of their counterparts in Germany, according to the international comparative study to be considered in more detail below. This eases the task faced by the teacher in Germany and accelerates progress. A school-leaving certificate is, in practice, the usual requirement for entry into any form of skilled occupation and provides motivation even for the academically less able.

The main contrasts with England at this broad level of discussion are first, that curricula and standards are set such that the great majority – about nine-tenths of all pupils – attain a school-leaving certificate; and, secondly, that minimum attainments are required in core subjects, depending on the level of the certificate. One wonders whether our system of allowing single subjects to be taken in final examinations and in separate years, provides a pupil with the right kind of incentives. If these features are to be retained, ought they not to be supplemented by a kind of grouped certificate, similar to the earlier Matriculation and School Certificate requirements?

Attainments in mathematics are clearly the easiest – or, more accurately, the least difficult – to compare between countries, and they are also of prime interest here because of the relevance to many technical and commercial occupations. Standards of school mathematics have for long been a source of serious worry in this country, leading eventually to the appointment of an official Committee of Inquiry under the chairmanship of Dr W. H. Cockroft; the Committee's report [*Mathematics Counts*, published at the end of 1981] gave disappointingly little attention to comparisons with attainments abroad. 'Our terms of reference', the Committee wrote blandly, 'have not required us to study the teaching of mathematics in other countries' [p.236]. There was no consideration of the international comparisons of mathematical attainments carried out by the International Educational Association (IEA) in which Britain, Germany and ten other countries took part [5]. Although that study was carried out in 1963-4, the data collected, which related to samples of many thousands of pupils at various ages, shed important light on the relative attainments of the different parts of the schooling systems of England and Germany. The main inferences are worth outlining here; as we shall see, subsequent comparisons indicate they are still fully relevant.

In brief, we learn from the IEA study that *mathematical attainments in England compared favourably with those in Germany at the top academic level* – for those who were mathematical specialists in the sixth forms of our Grammar schools; *but for the less able, those in English Secondary Modern schools, mathematical attainments at ages 13–14 compared very unfavourably with those in the corresponding German Main schools*. Taking a single figure for each country – to represent the average of all pupils together – does not therefore bring out the essence of our problem and this unevenness in relative attainments has perhaps been one reason why the British problem in mathematical schooling has not been attacked with greater vigour.

Part of the good side of this story is that the high attainments of those in mathematics and science sixth forms were recorded at average ages two years below comparable pupils in German schools (17 years 11 months in England and 19 years 10 months in Germany). German *Abitur* pupils took some ten subjects and, not surprisingly, did not attain the standards expected of our A-level pupils who usually take only three specialised subjects. The average mathematics score for the English A-level sample was 35 points in the IEA test, compared with an average of 29 points for Germany; there were some 70 questions in each of these broad-ranging tests.

The other side of the coin is less happy: the mathematical attainments of those of our A-level pupils not specialising in sciences or mathematics, who constitute the majority of university entrants, was lower in England than in Germany, (averages of 21 and 28 marks respectively). This difference is again to be attributed to the breadth of their 'sixth form' curriculum: all pupils in Germany hoping to proceed to a university take mathematics until the age of 18, as other core subjects. In consequence, the majority entering a university in Germany are better prepared in mathematics than in England; the 'higher innumeracy' and the split between the two cultures have not represented basic issues of educational philosophy in Germany as they have in England. Concerned as we are here with what is the best preparation for the workforce as a whole in a modern technological world, the German example supports the suggestion, recently put forward by our Think Tank, that grants for all university students be made conditional on passes in mathematics and English language [1].

From the point of view of school preparation for vocational training, we must concern ourselves with the mathematical attainments of the great bulk of pupils and especially those in the lower half of the ability range; here the IEA results indicated an extraordinary gap between our Secondary Modern schools and the German Main schools. This appeared from tests administered to samples of pupils aged 13–14, when school attendance is compulsory for everyone in virtually all countries. While the results are subject to reservations because of sampling problems that arose in practice, the gap is too large to be seriously in doubt; after adjusting for differences in age, the comparable average scores appear as 13 points for English Secondary Modern pupils and 22 points for Main school pupils in Germany. For each year of schooling at that age there is a gain of some 4.4 points. The lag of English Secondary Modern pupils behind their German counterparts can be said, on that basis, to be equivalent to some two years of schooling. Taking into account that German pupils start school a year later, the lag in *schooling* attainments is even longer. Another way of expressing the gap, which may seem less formidable, is to note that the average score attained by German pupils in the lower half of the ability range was close to the average of *all* English pupils in the full ability range; if only we could bring our lower half up to our present average, the gap would be closed.

To check on the current relative position we exchanged recent school-leaving test papers between mathematics teachers in the two countries. Our CSE 'mathematics' papers, which are intended for the *middle* range of pupils in England, were thought by German teachers to be quite appropriate in scope and difficulty for their Main school pupils, that is, for pupils in the *lower half* of the ability range in Germany. Going one step down in level of difficulty, CSE 'arithmetic' papers (which are simpler than CSE 'mathematics' papers, and may carry only lower grades) yielded the response from German teachers that these were distinctly below the level appropriate to their Main school leavers. Correspondingly, responses from teachers in England indicated that final-year tests at German Main schools were above the range of the corresponding streams in English Comprehensive schools. The tests administered in England annually since 1978 by the DES Assessment of Performance Unit to representative samples of pupils at age 15 provide the opportunity for more specific comparisons with pupils of similar age in Baden-Württemberg at their Main school leaving examination and these support the differences set out above.

Taking all the above together, we seem to have a broadly consistent picture of long-standing substantial lags in the mathematical attainments of our lower-half pupils behind Germany. Commentators who have pointed to inadequacies of this kind over many past decades were undoubtedly right: but the many remedial steps taken do not seem to have been effective. For example, the Report of the Schools Council in the late 1960s on *Mathematics for the Majority* was directed precisely to the issue of how to improve mathematics teaching for the less able – but the results of which fell into almost complete oblivion. And, why has the obvious measure of increasing openly and explicitly the relative salaries of mathematics teachers never been adopted?

At the beginning of 1984 the Secretary of State for Education and Science set as a target the raising of the general educational standards of all but the lowest fifth or tenth in this country to that of the present average; such a target would be consistent with present-day German attainments, at least in mathematics. In the light of our educational history, it remains, however, questionable whether our schooling 'system' is capable of responding without fundamental changes in curriculum development, in curriculum control, and in school management.

interests may be mentioned briefly: it is the progress made there in the teaching of vocational subjects. Four to eight school periods a week are dedicated to this group of subjects in the last four years at their Main schools by pupils in Berlin. Although this aspect of schooling has probably been developed further in Berlin than elsewhere, it will do no harm to take it as our example. The work carried out, for example, in electronic circuitry is at a remarkably high level, the authorised Berlin workbook including as choice of practice work construction of a telephone amplifier, burglar alarm and electronic metronome, all of which involve the preparation of printed circuits. Qualified master craftsmen are employed as full-time school staff to give instruction in such subjects. The aim has gone far beyond the older 'woodwork for boys, needlework for girls' to provide serious preparation for the world of work and for the subsequent courses at vocational schools on the day-release basis described above. Choice of career is aided by three-week spells at work in the penultimate school year.

Throughout these vocational courses there is an emphasis on commercial aspects, such as the preparation of costing sheets, discounts for buying components in bulk, and the need to find customers for the specimen articles produced by pupils. All this contrasts with the tendency to avoid practical and commercial elements in English schools where, for example, many local education authorities explicitly discourage commercial subjects, including type-writing, for school pupils under 16. It is thus hardly surprising that the modal German school leaver, when embarking on his traineeship at age 15–16, is better prepared than his English counterpart. The tasks of teachers at subsequent vocational schools are much eased because they can rely not only on higher average standards, but also on more even minimum standards.

There is much to be done. It will perhaps serve to emphasise the difficulty of doing it if I conclude by saying that, regretfully, I believe nothing in this paper is really new. A study of official educational reports will show that the facts represented here have been known, at least in general terms, for many decades; and the proposed policy measures I have ventured to suggest for discussion have been advanced many times before. A fundamental re-thinking of our 'system' is necessary.

References

[1] Central Policy Review Staff, *Education, Training and Economic Perform-ance*, HMSO, 1980, p.42.
[2] Eurostat Bulletin, *Unemployment*, December 1983. See also US Bureau of Labor Statistics, *Youth Unemployment: An International Perspective* (Bulletin 2098), September 1981; and *Supplement*, August 1982.
[3] Eurostat Bulletin, *Employment and Unemployment*, April 1983.
[4] Hollenstein, H., Economic performance and the vocational qualifications of the Swiss labour force compared with Britain and Germany, National Institute Discussion Paper no. 54, 1983.
[5] Husen, T. (ed), *International Study of Achievement in Mathematics*, vol. II, Almquist and Wiksell, Stockholm, 1967, p.81.
[6] *International Price Competitiveness, Non-price Factors and Export Perform-ance*, NEDO, 1977, Appendix C, especially the survey of many previous studies of non-price elements on pp. 37–44.
[7] *National Institute Economic Review*, August 1982 (special issue on Britain's comparative productivity), see especially p. 11.
[8] Prais, S.J., Daly, A, Jones, D.T. and Wagner, K., *Productivity and*

Industrial Structure, Cambridge University Press, 1981, chapter 19.

[9] Prais, S.J., Vocational qualifications of the labour force in Britain and Germany, *National Institute Economic Review*, November 1981.

[10] Prais, S.J. and Wagner, K., Some practical aspects of human capital investment: training standards in five occupations in Britain and Germany, *National Institute Economic Review*, August 1983.

[11] Prais, S.J. and Wagner, K., Schooling standards in Britain and Germany: some summary comparisons bearing on economic efficiency, National Institute Discussion Paper no. 60, July 1983.

[12] Sorge, A., Hartmann, G., Warner, M. and Nicholas, I., *Microelectronics and Manpower in Manufacturing*, Gower Publishing, 1983.

6 Developments in Vocational Training in France in the Past Twenty Years
by Alain d'Iribarne

France puts significant resources into its vocational and technical training systems, comparable with those of other European countries such as West Germany. More than 1.7 million young people are absorbed each year into an initial training programme with a highly articulated logic. Alongside the instruction programmes connected with the Education Department or technical ministries, such as Agriculture or Health, are the systems of training of apprentices and of adults and special programmes – of increasing importance recently – for youngsters who are no longer in the initial stages of training (see table 6.1).

Table 6.1   Personnel in vocational and technological training (by order of size in 1980/1), thousands

Second short cycle (vocational instruction lycées)	770
Second long cycle (technical lycées)	410
Apprenticeship	220
Higher technological training	90
Schools dependent on the Ministries of Health and Agriculture	190
AFPA	60
Army	40

Source: J. F. de Martel

In recent years important changes have taken place in French vocational and technical training, as well as in those branches of higher education which bear on technology. The latest measures concern training for young people within industry. The sum total of these developments is similar to that observed in other European countries faced with technological and economic development and crisis level unemployment. But they embody a distinct French way of thinking in the link between jobs and training, in the procedures followed, and in the programmes which are set up. These can be understood only within the framework of the previous French educational structure. To appreciate the full significance of the changes it is necessary to go back to the end of the 1950s and the early 1960s; at that time French governments laid the foundations of the present educational system and the links between general education and the vocational training systems.

As a result of the postwar increase in the number of children prolonging their education beyond primary level, the vocational training apparatus has been faced with three major problems: a) the need to produce qualified manpower to accompany (or, better, to precede) changes in the technical requirements of industry; b) the need to remedy the failures in the general education system which puts many young people on the labour market without adequate qualifications; and c) the need to face up to failure of the labour market which has led to a particularly large increase in youth unemployment. The first two continued largely unchanged, though taking different forms, during the whole period. The third has become more prominent in the current economic crisis.

These problems raise issues of an ideological nature: the quest for a parallel between the education system and the world of work, alternative combinations of theoretical and practical knowledge, and the changed basis for the socialisation of young people. The basic ideology of *alternance* – alternating periods of work and study throughout life – carried much weight in making detailed decisions on these issues.

A series of successive provisions resulted. Some were emergency *ad hoc* measures, others were of longer-term structural significance. They amount to a series of reforms which have gradually changed the whole role of vocational training in the French educational system. New responsibilities have fallen on the Minister for Education and the Minister for Vocational Training. The latter is a newly-created role in France; the Minister sees his responsibilities as being concerned with the arrangements for the school-to-work transition of young people. As a result of the industrial recession, many of the provisions appear to have become part of a permanent and relatively coherent framework, despite changes in ministerial teams and political majorities.

The main characteristics of the changes in the basic education system

Basic vocational and technical training in France is structured around a number of levels of training with corresponding certificates or diplomas ascending in technical level from craftsman to advanced technician. They are shown in table 6.2 (the English translations are inevitably very approximate). A total of 440,000 such vocational certificates were issued in 1981, compared with 161,000 *Baccalaureats* ('A' levels) in the same year. The present structure of diplomas and certificates is the result of a gradual restructuring of the educational system, marked by certain reforms of a more important kind which are described below.

Table 6.2   Levels of training, 1981

	Starting age	Type of school	Numbers issued ('000s)	Level of study (years)
Certificat d'Aptitude Professionelle (CAP)		Vocat-ional		
Certificate of Vocational Aptitude	14–16	secondary	248	3
Brevet d'Etudes Professionelles (BEP)		Vocat-ional		
Diploma in Vocational Studies	14 or 16	secondary	84	3
Brevet de Techniciens (BT)				
Technician's Certificate	17-18	Lycée	63	3
Baccalaureat de Technicien (BTn)				
Technician's Diploma	17-18	Lycée	5	3
Brevet de Techniciens Supérieurs (BTS)				2 after
Higher technician's certificate	post–16	Lycée	19	A-level
Diplome Universitaire de Technologie (DUT)		Univers-		2 after
University Diploma of Technology	post–16	ity	21	A-level

The setting up of a basic structure in the 1960s
As in all the European countries during the 1960s, the motivation behind the evolution of the education system lay in changes in the production system and the need for labour to adapt to changes in technology.

The 1959 reform constituted the basis of current systems of training. It lengthened compulsory school attendance to age 16 for pupils who began school in that year. (The lengthening of the school-leaving age to 16 therefore became effective in 1967, at which time these young people had reached the age of 14.) It created an 'observation cycle' of two years at the beginning of secondary education, which would normally include all pupils coming from primary classes. It therefore deferred entry into vocational and technical training until the end of this observation cycle.

The decrees of 1962 and 1963 created in effect the Colleges of Secondary Education (CES) in which are grouped the main educational channels. These divided secondary education into two distinct cycles. The most important aspect is that of the so-called 'Fouchet reform' which aimed at the abolition of those channels which led to the CAP in three years, and the deferment of entry into all technical training until after the third class. Provision was made for setting up preparatory stages of two years for the CAP to serve as a framework for stages preparatory to taking the BEP, which came into effect in 1969 as did the three-year preparatory stages for the BT.

The aim of these reforms was to prevent premature streaming of pupils, to democratise training/teaching and, especially, to raise the basic level of training of workers and professional employees. The emphasis placed in the Fourth Plan on the shortage of more highly qualified manpower also led to an insistence on the need to develop training at technician level. The first BTs prepared in technical schools were issued in 1966.

In 1965 a decree reforming the second long cycle fused general and technical training, in order to achieve parity between the different types of diploma to enable those who obtained them to continue at university, so attracting more young people. Therefore technicians' diplomas were created alongside the BTs, the first of which were awarded in 1969. In 1966 in the universities, Institutes of Technology (IUT) were established for higher technicians with the intention of substituting for the previous Higher Technicians Departments created in 1957. In 1967 the first BEP classes began, on an experimental basis, and the first pupils to attain this qualification finished their studies in 1970.

In one sense the evolution of the BTs towards the DUT and of the CAP towards the BEP are the results of the same basic logic, namely that vocational and technical training must cope with new activities resulting from the evolution of techniques and the organisation of work.

Changes in the 1970s: school and manual work
The 1970s brought new preoccupations. First of all a lengthening of the period of compulsory schooling does not necessarily improve the school-leaving standards of pupils and many young people ended up in the 'relegation channels' of the Pre-Vocational Level Classes (CPPN) and the Pre-Apprenticeship Classes. Education ministers, therefore, became concerned about academic failure. It was then observed that young people were facing increasing difficulties on leaving the education system; difficulties perceptible in the European Community since 1973. An early diagnosis attributed this situation to deficiencies in the preparation of young people. This resulted in the idea of creating a gradual transition from training to employment by forging closer links between education and business enterprises. It was intended that the number of pupils with low academic attainments finishing at the lower level V would have positive guidance and would be equipped with elements of vocational training. (It was only in 1978/9 that the increasing difficulties encountered by young people seeking employment began to be attributed as much to the general situation of the job market as to training deficiencies.) The emphasis moved towards the management of the transition between school and working life, especially for young people with no vocational training whose main

objective is the attainment of a steady job.

New guidelines were set out in 1971 with the initiation of vocational training at the end of the fifth class. In 1972/3 the CPPN and Pre-Apprenticeship Classes (CPA) replaced the third and fourth practical classes created in 1963. The aim of these new classes was to offer youngsters, still within the framework of compulsory schooling, the beginnings of vocational and general training in such a way as to allow them to make a choice of vocation under the best possible conditions and to make it easier for them to get a manual job. The form of apprenticeship was changed to a form of training which alternated between periods spent with master craftsmen and in Apprentice Training Centres (CFA), at which the corresponding theoretical knowledge was acquired. An apprenticeship could no longer start until after the end of the compulsory schooling period at the age of 16. However, this entry age was lowered to 15 in 1972 and to 14 in 1973, which brought the situation back to what it had been before 1971 (the Royer Act).

The CPPN and CPA classes, which were maintained at the time of the 1975 reform, functioned as relegation classes. In 1980 they catered for 170,000 pupils – 100,000 of these in CPPN – almost 17 per cent of the school population. The majority of young people who go into classes are the children of manual workers or of underprivileged categories like foreign workers and will have experienced difficulties at primary school. Likewise the CPAs encountered difficulties in that nearly 40 per cent could not find apprenticeship contracts when they finished their courses.

In 1975 the 'Haby Act', the provisions of which were to take effect in 1976, emphasised the division between the levels of the education system which equip each teaching cycle with a specific academic structure: the primary cycle corresponds to 'school', the first secondary cycle to 'college' and the second secondary cycle to 'Grammar school'. On the other hand the vocational training departments at the General Teaching Colleges (CET) have been regrouped into a single structure known as the School of Vocational Teaching (*Lycée d'Enseignement Professionel*) (LEP). The act intended that the CPPN and CPA classes should be replaced by preparatory classes attached to vocational training establishments offering technological options, with the objective of preparing certain pupils in the fourth and third classes for vocational training. However, these classes never came into effect.

The objective of the Haby Act was to revalue manual work so as to guide pupils at an early stage towards classes giving only a minimum of pre-vocational initiation but leading rapidly towards working life, while selecting the best pupils for higher levels. Since the higher-level structures were already established, maximum attention was therefore directed towards the pre-vocational initiation. With this end in mind, Manual and Technical Education (EMT) was introduced into colleges.

In December 1978 the *Conseil National du Patronat Français (CNPF)* (equivalent of the CBI) proposed the creation, under its responsibility, of Technical Vocational Institutes (ITP) which, based on the principle of alternating between periods of study and periods of practical experience and on teaching autonomy, would absorb pupils who had finished their compulsory schooling and give them a vocational course possibly leading to the CAP and the BEP. Undeniably the German model was starting to influence France, a model which itself was the object of reform in Germany in 1976, even while employment continued to rise there.

Between 1978 and 1980, the arrival of M. Beullac as Minister of Education reinforced the desire to reconcile school with manual work by the restoration of apprenticeship and the development of the principle of *alternance*, as well as the desire to educate workers in the new technological and economic realities. Thus the Legendre Act reaffirmed the need for an introduction at school to working life with the adoption of the principle of *alternance* in both the academic and non-academic fields. It is no longer simply a case of creating specialised training at the end of schooling but of creating an adaptable workforce.

M. Beullac negotiated with the CNPF and the biggest trade union in the education system (the FEN) to establish 'training periods in industry' for pupils. The following measures were to apply both to pupils from the colleges and to those from Grammar schools. Firstly, the EMT would be taught to all college pupils from the sixth to the third classes. Secondly, better links between basic training and further training would be developed, with an ever increasing participation from professionals. Finally, young people aged 16–18 would be able to re-enter the education system in order to take up training activities.

The proposed law on *alternance* envisaged three types of alternated training in the form of three statutes: a) the school or university statute: the young person receives a grant during his period in the enterprise; b) the trainee vocational training statute: the periods of instruction include some time in an enterprise during which time trainees must carry out a task corresponding to their training: they are paid by the State; c) the wage-earner statute: the young person earning a wage could benefit from training organised by the State during working hours. The contract could be linked to an apprenticeship contract and both general and technological training would last from 500 to 2,000 hours. This training would lead to a particular job or a qualification certified by a recognised diploma.

Explicitly intended to combat youth unemployment and lack of training, this project was abandoned as a result of opposition by the unions of both manual workers and teaching staff. The only provisions put into practice since 1979 are: educational periods in enterprises limited to LEP and on an experimental basis; and time spent in enterprises for colleges and schools. Four complementary measures have been taken: better induction methods for pupils into areas of technological knowledge; an improvement of information in the same establishments; an increase in general training in technical areas; and a reinforcement of the role of enterprises in education on a national basis.

The early 1980s: the fight against unemployment and for competitiveness in the future

At the beginning of the 1980s, before the Socialists came to power, the general direction of the education system took a new turn. New measures were worked out to take effect at the start of the 1980/1 academic year. They were designed to raise the level of technological training within the education system to make available the human potential considered necessary for the restructuring of the French economy.

a) It was planned to apply measures for the speedy identification of pupils encountering difficulties in the top two classes of primary school (CM1 and CM2).

b) Fourth and third preparatory classes were set up, not as a substitute for the CPPN and CPA classes, as the Haby reform had intended, but to raise over the three years the number of hours of general education in the first and second years of the CAP to bring pupils closer to the students in fourth and third classes in the colleges.

c) The EMT and the technological options were recast, not only for the fourth and third classes, but also for the sixth and fifth, with the object of inculcating not only a simple perception capability, but also the ability to work out concepts and to think at a technological level.

d) New technological choices with a more cultural than vocational bias were introduced, not in order to syphon off pupils towards the LEPs, but to provide technical qualifications.

e) New, non-specialising, second classes (that is, penultimate-year) were also introduced, with the object of extending to all stages some of the basic technological knowledge provided at the outset in stages leading specifically to the technician's diploma.

The new government's policy, which emerged through the 1982–3 interim plan and the policies of the Ninth Plan (1984–8) is in line with previous policies, but lays more stress on combating failure at school. On the one hand, the bridging classes (second special and first adjustment) were to be increased so that studies might be more readily continued after the CAP and the BEP towards the long technological training; the forging of links between schools and industry through

Educational Action Plans (PAEs) was to continue; and most important was the setting up in July 1981 of Educational Priority Zones (ZEPs) designed to combat inequality in education through an intensification of action in those social strata where the rate of school failures is the highest. In December 1981, a more broadly-based attack on school failures was announced through a determination to recast the Schools of Vocational Teaching; to offer clearer options at the end of the second class and to modify guidance procedures in the first years in the colleges.

The results of the changes

Whilst much remains to be done in view of the extent of pupil failure shown by the numbers who still end up in the relegation channels, the steady increase in the numbers receiving vocational and technological training bears witness to the efforts already undertaken.

The whole system of relegation channels has been operating at full stretch since, in 1981–2, it accounted for 310,000 pupils. In recent years numbers leaving without full vocational training have tended to drop, both in relative and in absolute terms, if one includes apprenticeship in basic training. They fell from 233,200 in 1974 to 99,200 in 1979, but then rose slightly to 101,800 in 1980. Conversely, those leaving from levels V and IV increased greatly whilst the total of those leaving higher education went up slightly.

There has been a considerable increase in numbers of both teachers and students gaining diplomas in vocational and technological

Table 6.3   Increase in numbers of diplomas awarded between 1970 and 1980

		1970	1975	1979	1980
Level V:	CAP	183,352	200,589	235,667	235,046
	BEP	28,493	58,854	79,046	78,905
	Total[b]	211,845	259,443	314,723	313,951
Level IV:[a]	BT	7,442	3,451	4,585	4,521
	Tech. A level	28,600	50,804	61,009	62,660
	Total	36,022	54,225	65,594	17,101
Level III:	BTS	10,463	11,526	17,101	17,442
	DUT	6,482	14,746	18,645	19,769
	Total	16,945	26,272	35,746	37,211

Source: F. Meylan, 'Evolution des formations dans les spécialités mécaniques et connexes (y compris l'électronique) de 1955 à 1980', CEREQ, multigraphie, Paris, June 1984.

[a] Not including the BP sociology diploma.

[b] It must be remembered that this is the number of *diplomas*; at level V, a pupil can gain several diplomas.

teaching. In the ten years between 1970 and 1980, the numbers achieving diplomas from technical courses have almost doubled, BEPs have trebled, as also have DUTs.

In fact, however, these increases largely result from tertiary training. This is particularly true at level IV, where the number of industrial diplomas rose by only 16.2 per cent between 1965 and 1980. Likewise, between 1970 and 1980, numbers in final industrial classes for IUTs and STSs doubled.

To achieve real success, there should have been a more fundamental change in the quality of this teaching, taking into account the changes which have occurred in the open or closed stages and the content of the instruction provided. That is beyond the scope of this chapter.

Post-school vocational training for young people

Intended, in principle, to strengthen measures designed to develop the basic education system, post-school vocational training for young people actually had ambivalent objectives. First, it was to limit the deterioration in the unemployment statistics by keeping young people in the education system. Secondly, it appeared to counter the enormous wastage resulting from the failure of the education system in the primary classes and the first cycle of secondary education. Thirdly, it would apply a brake to the very high numbers of young people leaving school on reaching the end of compulsory education without any vocational training. Fourthly it would provide industry with cheap, temporary, labour for unimportant work under cover of an employment training label. Preparing for the future by establishing vocational and technological training would therefore enable those concerned to acquire a high level of vocational ability through theoretical and practical knowledge obtained by alternating the two types of training.

As before, the year 1980 was a turning point, marking a distinct stage in the establishment of the French post-school training system for young people. Leaving aside all the July 1971 laws, which concerned all adults in apprenticeship or at the AFPA, our central concern will be with the various measures taken at the prompting of the Employment and Vocational Training Delegations (Government departments) and subsequently of the Office of the Secretary of State and the Ministry for Vocational Training, which began to take shape in 1977.

1977–81: The employment pacts

From 1975 onwards the public authorities began to take measures designed to help young people to enter employment. But it was not until 1977 that, faced with mounting unemployment, a system known as the National Employment Pact was set up. This pact, which applied to a wider group than just young people, was originally intended to last one year and was twice extended with provisions which, despite modifications to the legislative texts and regulations, retained their general structure basically unchanged.

The first pact (July 1977–July 1978) applied to those under 25 who had completed their education or military service less than one year previously. The second pact (July 1978–July 1979), which was also designed as a short-term measure, applied to those between the ages of 16 and 18 who had completed a course of technological education and to those between 18 and 20 who had completed their training or military service less than one year previously. The third pact, spread over two and half years (July 1979–December 1981), was from the outset a more structural measure. Including women, like the previous one but on a wider basis, it also applied to the long-term unemployed over the age of 45.

In addition to incentives to industry, such as social security contribution exemptions of greater or lesser value, the pacts included measures aimed at the acquisition or improvement of vocational training. These were principally of three types: employment/training contracts, vocational preparatory courses and practical courses within industry.

The *employment/training contracts* already introduced in 1975 were normal work contracts of six months' or one year's duration. Employers undertook to provide their holders with in-service training under an agreement signed between the State and the employer. There were two categories of contract: entry-into-employment contracts consisting of between 120 and 500 hours' training, designed to assist adaptation to a job or to obtain an additional qualification, and the so-called 'qualification contracts' consisting of between 500 and 1200 hours' training designed to enable unqualified young people to obtain a qualification.

The *vocational preparatory courses* were also set up for the first time in 1975. They too provided both practical and vocational training of less than six months' duration involving a maximum of 800 hours' attendance at a training centre and at least four week's applied work in industry. Trainees received a lump sum payment.

The *practical courses* within industry lasted four months. They were designed to enable young people without vocational qualifications to obtain their first experience of the world of work and so gain practical awareness to help them to decide which direction to take. Vocational training students received an allowance from the State whilst, up to a certain limit, the firm could deduct expenditure on the course from the payment of the vocational tax. These courses are normally required to include 120 hours' theoretical vocational training complementary to the activity involved throughout the course. At its conclusion, the young person might be recruited into the firm, or he could continue with a vocational preparatory course, leading in certain circumstances to an employment/training contract.

The principal results

After a slow start, the employment/training contracts have increased steadily with a marked preference for the third pact. Slightly more than half of these contracts, which mainly benefited boys, were signed by industrial firms including more than 50 per cent employing less than 50 workers. In the majority of cases (81 per cent), the duration of training was less than 500 hours, whilst too many posts filled were at the lowest level.

The numbers of vocational preparatory courses have dropped steadily from the first to the last pact: from 68,000 to 38,000 trainees. Whilst available statistics on the type of trainees in the first campaign for the second pact show that they correspond to the target population, there continued to be few untrained young people (24 per cent) whereas the proportion of those having a level of education equal to or better than A-levels was nearly one-third.

The development of these practical courses has been uneven, with a large drop during the first campaign for the third pact and especially during the second pact. These courses were better received by the tertiary sectors than the employment/training contracts. Young people trained to level V were the first beneficiaries, but the higher levels were widely represented.

The few reports on the results of the pacts conclude that their essential role has been to avoid the waves of young people annually entering the labour market, but that they have scarcely created any jobs (about 5,000 per annum). On the other hand, contrary to the

Table 6.4   *Distribution of the various measures by employment pact, thousands*

	Pact I 1.7.77–31.3.78	Pact II 1.7.78–31.3.79	Pact III 1.7.79–30.6.80	1.7.80–31.3.81
Apprenticeship	108.3	103.9	122.5	120.3
Exemptions	229.9	95.0	151.6	118.9
Practical courses	145.7	20.3	55.3	140.3
Employment/training contracts	26.4	38.1	64.3	47.3
Training courses	68.7	55.9	46.2	38.4
Total	579.0	313.2	439.9	465.2

Source: M. Figeat, 'Politique de formation de la main d'oeuvre en France: Aspects principaux (1975–1983)', Institut National de la Recherche Pédagogique, Paris, December 1983.

announced purposes of the pacts, they have been of benefit to untrained young people, PMEs tending to use young people as cheap manpower, not as students under training. However, the employment/training contracts produced better results since, in 1978, six months after they ended, some 85 per cent of those concerned were retained in their firms, against 62 per cent from the practical courses and 50 per cent from the training courses. Thus the practical courses turned out to be a poor alternative.

Since 1980: the 'Avenir Jeunes' (future for youth) and 'Mesures 16–18 ans' (Measures for the 16–18s) plans

As has been seen, the bill on alternating vocational training claimed to have the very broad aim of introducing *alternance* into all fields and at all levels of training. It was aimed at people seeking employment, whatever their age and level of diploma and at wage earners of up to 23. It proposed two types of training: adjustment or preparation for employment leading to a diploma and training for qualifications also leading to a diploma of technical education or a certificate of acknowledged qualification.

The Eighth Plan, which was not ratified by Parliament, had called for a five-year plan to 'facilitate entry into employment and improve the qualification of young people' with Priority Action Programme No. 4. The aim of this programme was to provide satisfactory vocational training and employment for all young people, by ensuring that the training provided corresponded properly to the social needs of the country. This programme was to apply to all young people at the end of their training: at the conclusion of compulsory training, with contracts for alternating training of between six months and two years; to those leaving the second general training cycle or the higher level with alternating training of one year; and those leaving vocational training with work contracts from one to three years designed to develop high level qualifications. In addition to the development of apprenticeship, Alternating Vocational Training Sections would have been set up, with the object of giving all young people a first qualification within the one-year training.

Since the proposals for alternating vocational training and the provisions laid down in the Eighth Plan came to nothing, the provisions of the third employment pact were extended until July 1982, in the expectation of a new in-depth reform designed to provide greater stability of employment for those covered by the plan and a higher degree of priority for young people with no vocational training. The changes relate mainly to the employment/training contracts and the practical courses in industry, the numbers of which were reduced from 140,000 to 50,000. They concern the manner in which the State undertakes responsibility for social (security) contributions. Additionally, since local authorities can participate on the same basis as private industry, the minimum age for employment/training contracts in craft industries was lowered from 20 to 18 whilst the average duration of the training was increased from 380 hours to 444 and the guaranteed period of employment doubled, rising from 6–12 months to 12–24 months.

In practice, the *Avenir Jeunes Plan* consists of: a) vocational preparatory courses which replaced the training courses and were aimed both at qualifying courses lasting five to eight months with 800 hours' training and introduction-to-employment courses lasting 800 to 1,200 hours; b) vocational experience courses which replaced the practical courses which were to be discontinued at the conclusion of the plan on 30 June 1982; c) employment/training contracts involving on the one hand introduction-to-employment courses designed to provide job experience and lasting more than one year, with between 120 and 500 hours' training and, on the other, qualifying contracts designed to give a vocational qualification to those having none and lasting more than 24 months, with between 500 and 1,200 hours' training.

Whilst the aim of the system was to reach 620,000, 100,000 of them for employment/training contracts and 50,000 for vocational preparatory courses, by December 1981 only 296,500 had been reached and industry continued to prefer practical courses and to be unenthusiastic about social security exemptions.

On the basis of a report by Professor B. Schwartz submitted in September 1981, the new government set up for the second half of 1982 a new programme of vocational qualification and entry into the social system for those between 16 and 18. The aim was to ensure that no young person in this age group should enter the labour market without having acquired vocational training resulting in the award of a diploma.

Three types of action were foreseen; a) reception, information and guidance provided mainly by the Reception, Information and Direction Services (PAIO). These services were partly financed from the vocational training and social improvement fund and were brought into being through agreements with local authorities or through 'Local Missions' which were more solid organisations. Their purpose was to inform young people and direct them towards opportunities for beginning training. b) In-depth guidance designed to assist young people whose inclination would make it difficult for them to start working for a qualification likely to lead to social improvement. c) Alternating training measures in private or national firms. These training measures were originally the same thing as the introduction-to-employment courses as defined within the framework of the *Avenir Jeunes Plan* and as 8–month qualifying training courses in which 50 per cent of the time was spent in industry.

The setting up of the system involved a combination of opportunities to inform, direct and train so that the young person was, as it were, guided towards a vocational qualification. For example, he could have a collective starter module of 20 hours followed by a qualifying course; or an in-depth collective guidance course of 120 hours followed by a week in industry and then a qualifying course; or, finally, a social and vocational entry course followed by a similar qualifying course or any other solution.

In November 1983, a first assessment of the system showed that 167,000 young people had been received by the 812 PAIOs and the 87 local missions set up, whilst 92,000 had undertaken courses (half of them entry courses; one-third qualification courses and one-fifth in-depth guidance) and 28,000 had preferred direct employment, a return to apprenticeship or to the education system. It was also observed that the system had not been in competition with traditional training facilities but that there were, within it, considerable distortions detrimental to girls. Another big problem concerned terms of employment on leaving the system, which did not appear very favourable, in view of the state of the labour market. This is a particularly worrying state of affairs when young people claim that, above all, they want work.

At the end of the *Avenir Jeunes Plan*, the various systems were adjusted in a number of ways. Thus, practical courses were abolished, as was the exemption granted by the State of 50 per cent of the employer's contribution, whereas assistance negotiated with industry was encouraged. In addition, entry-into-employment courses for the 18–21s which followed on the former entry and qualifying courses under the Avenir Jeunes Plan were introduced to follow the measures for the 16–18s. Finally, the employment/training contracts were revived. So, in May 1983, the system of contracts was recast to introduce: a) employment/training contracts for 18–26s who were encountering difficulties in entering the world of work; they are a continuation of the previous entry and qualifying contracts which bore the same title; b) employment/adjustment contracts for unemployed but qualified 16–26s; these are contracts of a minimum of one year's duration of which 180 hours are paid for by the State; c) employment/direction contracts for untrained job-seekers among the 18–26s. These contracts are for at least four months' duration. They are designed to enable young people to attend assessment and direction sessions arranged at ANPE or AFPA. State aid accounts for 80 hours.

In 1982/3 the number of young people reached was 80,000. The aim for 1983/4 is 200,000. An ambitious aim!

Broadly, the objective, following the abolition of the Avenir Jeunes Plan, is to have an overall training system aimed first and foremost at all the misfits from the education system and making it possible to lead them gradually to training culminating in the qualification of a vocational training diploma. That is why current plans for reform include continuing vocational training with better supervision of the six months to two years qualifying contracts for the 18–26s and improved continuity between initial training and follow-up training.

Conclusion

A chronological approach has been adopted in this chapter to clarify (a) the changes in the educational system and in basic training made by the Ministry for Education; and (b) the post-schooling measures put into effect by what is now the Ministry for Vocational Training. We have emphasised the legislative and institutional aspects, explaining the contents of successive legal statutes and mentioning only briefly statistical and pedagogical aspects. Such an approach revealed the objectives of policy as much by the reforms put into effect as by those avoided.

The recession has resulted in a multiplicity of reforms. They have often succeeded each other at such speed that they have tended partly to overlap and partly to cancel each other out, making difficult any simple evaluation. The increase in the power of the Ministry of Vocational Training is very noticeable. It first used provisional measures and then gradually created conditions for an institutionalisation of the transition between school and work. These aimed at variety and flexibility, having regard to local and industrial needs; steps have been taken towards a partial decentralisation of education, and vocational training has begun to move towards a decentralised system. From this point of view France is following a path already trodden by other countries like Great Britain and Italy. A succession of problems has been faced in relation to changes in production methods, the need to produce qualified personnel allowing for a changing division of labour and the need to react to unemployment.

From this last point of view it seems legitimate to worry about the adverse effects of measures taken in 1982 aimed to restrict young people to temporary work and work-contracts of a fixed (short) duration. The risk is that this scheme will be used as a normal route which the majority of young people must follow at the end of the school system before having the right ultimately to secure adult employment. According to current estimates of recruitment of young people, it appears that almost half of all youngsters recruited in 1984 will have a short-term contract and a further 20 per cent will be subject to uncertain rights. This shows once again how, irrespective of good intentions, the realities of the labour market dominate the actual situation.

On the other hand, the current measures can be seen as part of an inevitable transition towards a future in which a restructured educational system will play an essential role. This is clearly evident from the guidelines issued by the Programme Prioritaire d'Execution No. 2 of the Ninth Plan which envisages the utilisation of the equivalent of £8 billion in the next four years for restructuring the education and training system, a third of which will be used for vocational and social placement. The aim by 1988 is to reduce by half the number of young people leaving school without qualifications.

As far as the educational system is concerned, it will be a question of changing vocational colleges, and changing technical and vocational instruction; there will be a trend towards longer courses of the IUT type, and more school pupils will stay on to the equivalent of the sixth form. For the post-school training stages a reduction of the duration of *alternance* for young people aged 16–18 is envisaged; more emphasis will be given to training contracts providing combined instruction and on-the-job training, particularly aimed to help those finishing school without qualifications. The stakes remain high.

7 A Comparison of the Youth Training Scheme in the United Kingdom with the Vocational Foundation Training Year in Germany
by Russ Russell

In all of Western Europe, while the pace of technological change has increased in the last decade or so, the economies have hesitated and faltered. The common result has been a general rise in the level of youth unemployment, both for young people entering the vocational education and training systems and for those young people seeking further employment after an initial training. Few experts care to attempt to predict future patterns of employment, nor to assert what that employment might need by way of skills. Most are mindful not only of a steady European-wide decline in employment in manufacturing but also that all occupations are experiencing rapid change of content arising from a range of new technologies but, above all, cheap data-processors and micro-computers.

One reaction to the difficulties of training for the future has been a move towards broad-based polyvalent training in generic or transferable skills. In this context there seem to be interesting parallels between the *Berufsgrundbildungsjahr* (BGJ-Vocational Foundation Training Year) in Germany and the Youth Training Scheme (YTS) in the United Kingdom. Both appear to move towards broad-based training in generic skills. Is there anything to be learned from comparing the two? Are there any long-term curriculum lessons? Does research justify the curriculum theory that there are such generic skills, what they are and how to teach them? What effect does the possession of these generic skills subsequently have on employment and learning capacity? [1] Such research on a comparative basis must alas wait because the YTS is so new in the United Kingdom. On the other hand, there is already the possibility of making tentative remarks on the basis of a comparison of policy formulation and implementation that are of interest.

Berufsgrundbildungsjahr (BGJ)
The BGJ has a considerable history already being (in conception) nearly fifteen years old. Perspectives on the justification of the experiment vary both over time and with the partners involved in the change.

Manfred Kaiser (1977) has summed them up as providing or facilitating:

(a) room for manoeuvre prior to selection of a specific occupation within the *Berufsfeld* (Vocational Field) selected;

(b) an initial taster experience to be obtained;

(c) a streamlining in the presentation of basic content to take place;

(d) the broad occupational base necessary for potential advancement to higher qualifications (or for transfer to other occupations) to be provided;

(e) the participants to enjoy more flexibility in the work situation and enhance their opportunity to change jobs.

In Germany at the time of the initial experiments, most young people who left school at the minimum age entered an apprenticeship in one of the 460 or so training trades recognised in Germany. They receive, in these apprenticeships, both systematic on-the-job training and also day-release for vocational and general education (a system known as the Dual System). At the end there is an examination for skilled status and most young people will have access after that to further qualification routes leading to Master, Technician or Administrator (*Betriebswirt/ Fachwirt*)[2]. The dual system is a respected system often held in folk-myth (and also perhaps reality) to be the basis of quality in the German economy and supporting the economic miracle of the 1950s and 1960s. This system has actually expanded over the last fifteen years and now encompasses more young people, and a greater proportion of young people than ever before [3].

Thus in order for the BGJ experiment to succeed, it had to be seen as an attractive alternative to this respected dual system. In practice it was necessary to incorporate it into the dual system in the following way. Trades within the dual system were analysed for training content, analysed as being networks of mutual recruitment etc after qualification and then put into clusters or *Berufselder* (vocational fields) (see also Appendix 7A). From the content analysis a common first year was derived for each cluster or sub-cluster and this is in essence the BGJ. In practice the clusters are based on material and tools (for example, metal, wood, food). If the BGJ is to be taught, all the three social partners must agree at a national level that a BGJ undertaken by a young person is acceptable and necessarily gains credit as being the equivalent of a first year apprenticeship for *any* of the trades in the vocational field [4].

The necessary agreements were reached but with differing significance for the partners. Traditional apprenticeships are defined in skill terms and also knowledge terms only as end-tests after three or so years.

Neither the employers nor the trade unions cared to attempt this for a first year and in the end the BGJ is defined only in educational terms and thus only the state was fully committed to it in terms of agreeing its content. The employers even at national level made no definition of skill content and insisted that the experiment was voluntary and thus undertook no obligation to 'deliver their members' in a corporatist way. The employers' organisations further distanced themselves on the non-delivery of the 'cooperative' form. The experiment was agreed to take place as both school (college) based, or in cooperation with industry. In practice only the state authorities pursued the experiment with any vigour. By 1983 there were 83,036 young people on the school-based form and only 15,861 on all 'cooperative' forms. It is interesting to note that in five of the agreed thirteen vocational fields there were no BGJ trainees in cooperative schemes by 1983 [5]. Initially the trade unions had favoured the school-based form as providing more and better general education but of course they cannot 'deliver' that since they have no training capacity. Later the metal workers union stated it preferred the cooperative form because they could not express opinions in the schools. Partly as a result of this exceptional attitude half (in 1983, 7,732) of all the cooperative forms exist in the single vocational field of *Metall* (Engineering).

The employers at a local level are also widely reported as having three main techniques of avoiding the nationally agreed creditworthiness [6] of the BGJ in school form:

(a) never to recruit from the BGJ;

(b) to recruit just before completion, the trainees thus having no legal credit;

(c) to suggest towards the end of the probationary period that the apprentice should request a voluntary extension of the (reduced?) apprenticeship.

No accurate data exist on the extent of their success in this. The employers have, by and large, continued to prefer and to provide, without state financial support, their traditional training. Thus the BGJ in school form is diminished in function to being an expanding holding-pool for surplus, but aspirant, potential apprentices. That seems to be its economic and labour market function. Its curriculum success is not discussed here [1]. Inevitably though, to the extent that it fulfills functions as a holding-pool it will attract young people who were not the first choice of the employers. It becomes difficult to separate out the effect of this selecting from any strength or weakness in its design.

The Youth Training Scheme

In contrast to Germany the United Kingdom has seen a relatively complete collapse of its traditional system of training as employers have abandoned it in the recession. Whereas about 85 per cent of all minimum-age school-leavers in Germany receive an apprenticeship in the dual system that figure is now about 6 to 8 per cent in the United Kingdom with perhaps a further 10 per cent on a comparable systematic training not necessarily protected by a contract. In the face of acute job uncertainty the Manpower Services Commission (MSC) has been instructed to provide one-year initial foundation training for all that require it commencing in the school year 1983–4. Their technical problem has been to decide what skills, since employment prospects are poor. Unlike their counterparts in Germany, the MSC has been relatively free from the need for corporate decision or commitment to it for it has to produce not a market substitute for an acceptable product, but an acceptable product where none exists. They have been able to allow the design around certain principles of transferability in which the trainees are made aware of their own skill ownership and its transferability. The technique has been to group occupations into Occupational Training Families (OTFs) (see Appendix 7B). In each OTF the principle has been not abstraction from respected training, but the generation of the *purpose* of an occupation in the mind of the individual trainee and that as the *theme* of relating the 'owned skills' to the available occupations (work).

This approach creates a facility for transferring owned-skills from one occupation to another by allowing the trainee to grasp the purpose of the occupation [7]. This OTF/Purpose approach is based on process rather than materials, tools or skills and thus makes major demands on the analytic and pedagogic skills of the training force who are forced to revise nearly all their existing pedagogic practice.

As a matter of strong ideological, as well as training and cost, preferences the Government hopes to keep the trainees close to 'real-work', which necessitates employers providing the places. Since the commitment was to a massive provision of over 460,000 places (more than industry had ever trained), employer commitment was essential. In practice only 354,000 places were taken by trainees – a nevertheless astonishing number in the first year of a new scheme[8]. This is provided firstly by money and secondly by the agreement that the design of the programmes lies with the employers (or managing agents)[9]. It remains to be seen if industry has the flexible trainers necessary to deliver the reality of such an ambitious new scheme, but the commitment is available from the employers without vast national negotiations.

Also what is needed to deliver is the cooperation or non-resistance of the trade unions at plant level and the cooperation of the technical colleges (and their controlling local education authorities) which may be involved in part of the delivery. In practice both have little power to resist, in the current financial climate. Nor is such resistance rational where the training provided can be seen as extra and not substituting for older, longer or better training. Local resistance is reduced to areas where traditional training is being removed. Incorporation has taken place by the establishment of a national Contents and Standards committee which, it is likely, by involving the national-level officials and elected-members of the trade unions, will create a management pressure within the unions to 'deliver'.

In certain traditional craft areas (such as building) a compromise has been reached whereby within national agreements involving the employers, the craft unions and the industrial training boards, the traditional first year training has been very little modified but expanded in numbers and financed as part of the YTS (but freed from many of its design principles).

The problem that arises is this: is the YTS year within its OTFs *really* an acceptable substitute for previous patterns of training? Will all find that it leads to and is the foundation for useful *second-year* training? It will be interesting to monitor this issue by mapping the *ad hoc* agreements within trades, within sectors or industries to see what patterns of cooperation and incorporation occur.

This chapter has necessarily skirted around the issues of training design, curriculum content and the skills of the training force in comparing the BGJ to the YTS. It has been an attempt to map the relationship of the participants in implementing two foundation training schemes and in that review to see the implications of the patterns of incorporation. The conclusion is that little further development in quantity or design is easy in the BGJ because of (a) the complex balance of forces in the corporatist net, and (b) the existence of a successful alternative. The YTS, however, is capable of significant qualitative improvement as a result of research, revision and development because (a) there is no balance of forces in the corporatist net (power lies with the government for quantity and the MSC for quality and content), and (b) there is generally no viable alternative (but where there is, then the balance in corporatist forces moves the YTS back towards traditional alternatives).

APPENDIX 7A

BGJ – VOCATIONAL AREAS AND SUB-DIVISIONS

I   WIRTSCHAFT UND VERWALTUNG –
    Business and Administration
    a)   ABSATZWIRTSCHAFT UND KUNDENBERATUNG

Marketing, Distribution, Servicing

b) BÜROWIRTSCHAFT UND KAUMÄNNISCHE
VERWALTUNG
Office Management and Business Administration

c) RECHT UND ÖFFENTLICHE VERWALTUNG
Law and Public Administration

II METALLTECHNIK – Metal Trades

a) FERTIGUNGS – UND SPANNENDE
BEARBEITUNGSTECHNIK
Production Engineering and Machining

b) INSTALLATIONS – UND METALLBAUTECHNIK
Fitting and Metal Construction

c) KRAFTFAHRZEUGTECHNIK
Motor Vehicle Engineering

III ELEKTROTECHNIK – Electrical Trades

IV BAUTECHNIK – Construction Trades
(Trowel Trades and Concrete)

V HOLZTECHNIK – Woodworking Trades
Carpentry, Joinery, Wood Machinists)

VI TEXTILTECHNIK UND BEKLEIDUNG –
Textiles and Garments

VII CHEMIE, PHSYSIK UND BIOLOGIE –
Laboratory and Science Based Process Work

VIII DRUCKTECHNIK -- Printing Technology

a) Laboratoriumstechnik – Laboratory Technology

b) Produktionstechnik – Production Technology

IX FARBTECHNIK UND RAUMGESTALTUNG –
Painting and Decorating

X GESUNDHEIT – Health

XI KÖRPERPFLEGE – Hairdressing and Beauty Therapy

XII ERNÄRUNG UND HAUSWIRTSCHAFT –
Food and Domestic Science

a) Catering and Domestic Work

b) Food Processing

c) Butchery

XIII   AGRARWIRTSCHAFT – Agriculture
   a)   Animal Husbandry
   b)   Crops

Source: Russell, R. and Parkes, D. L. (eds), Career development education in the FRG, Further Education Staff College, Blagdon, Avon, 1984.

APPENDIX B

OCCUPATIONAL TRAINING FAMILIES (OTFs) AND THEIR KEY PURPOSES

OTF No.	OCCUPATIONS	KEY PURPOSE
1	Administrative, clerical and office services	Information processing
2	Agriculture, horticulture, forestry and fisheries	Nurturing and gathering living resources
3	Craft and design	Creating single or small numbers of objects using hand/power tools
4	Installation, maintenance and repair	Applying known procedures for making equipment work
5	Technical and scientific	Applying known principles to making things work/usable
6	Manufacturing and assembly	Transforming metallic and non-metallic materials through shaping, constructing and assembling into products
7	Processing	Intervening into the working of machines when necessary
8	Food preparation and service	Transform and handle edible matter
9	Personal services and sales	Satisfying the needs of individual customers
10	Community and health services	Meeting socially defined needs of the community
11	Transport services	Moving goods and people

Source: Hayes, C. *et al*, Training for Skill Ownership, Institute of Manpower Studies, University of Sussex, 1983.

References

[1] Some evidence that the BGJ is a successful system of creating flexible learning skills is contained in the reports of the pilot schemes at Salzgitter: Weissker, D. *et al, Erprobung schulischer Berufsgrundbildung in Abstimmung mit der betrieblichen Fachbildung*, Bundesinstitut für Berufsbildung, Berlin, 1979; and also in the early reports of the 'cooperative' from Gerds, P. and Glaser, P., *Modellversuchen zum BGJ in kooperativer Form*, Bundesinstitut für Berufsbildung, Berlin, 1978.

[2] For further comments on this aspect of the Dual System see Russell, R. and Parkes, D. L. (eds), *Career development education in the FRG*, Further Education Staff College, Blagdon, Avon, 1984.

[3] The actual number of new contacts has varied a little over the last year or so. It has averaged 650,000 over the last three years compared with approximately 500,000 a decade ago: BMBW, *Grund- und Strukturdaten 1983–1984*, Bundesministerium für Bildung und Wissenschaft, Bonn, 1983.

[4] Two other commentaries on the BGJ easily available are those of the Federal Ministry: BMBW, *Bürger–Information: Berufsgrundbildungsjahr*, Bundesministerium für Bildung und Wissenschaft, Bonn, 1979.

[5] These figures are taken from Glaser, P. and Schmidt-Hackenberg, *Das BGJ im Schuljahr 1982/83*, Bundesinstitut für Berufsbildung, Berlin, 1984.

[6] See also Russell, R. and Neale, M. (eds), *Experiments with the first year of apprenticeships in the FRG* (second edition), Further Education Staff College, Blagdon, Avon, 1983. This report of a party of experts on vocational education and training in the United Kingdom provides an interesting commentary on the BGJ from an independent position.

[7] This is elaborated in Hayes, C. *et al, Training for skill ownership*, Institute of Manpower Studies, University of Sussex, 1983: a seminal report especially commissioned by the MSC for the purpose of creating curriculum design.

[8] MSC, *Manpower Memo, 83/84: Youth Training Scheme*, Manpower Services Commission, London and Sheffield, 1984.

[9] Not all Managing Agents are employers; some are local authorities. Well over 200,000 of the provided places were with employers.

Comment on Chapters 3–5
by Professor Maurice Peston

It shows no disrespect to the authors of these chapters when I say that
they contain very little that is new. They are well aware of this
themselves. This suggests two immediate comments, one optimistic
and one pessimistic. The former is that we know what to do, so let us go
ahead and do it. The latter is that we have always known what to do;
therefore, there must be very deep reasons why the problems persist. In
other words, what we are discussing here today is merely one part of the
general 'What is wrong with Britain?' question.

I must also at the outset make two rather broad methodological
remarks. *A priori* there is every reason to believe that there are
connections between education and the economy, each influencing and
being influenced by the other. This does not mean that the connection
is always and everywhere satisfactory. What I mean by this is twofold:
first, each may affect the other, but not in a good way; second, the
signals going from each to the other and the subsequent responses may
be highly imperfect.

To concentrate on the case in point, existing provision may actually
be damaging to the economy. To expand it and to allow it to influence
the economy more would then do more harm than good. In fact, we do
not know either way. My reading of the published literature leaves me
rather sceptical about education's actual achievements as opposed to
what it might do for economic performance. I believe strongly that it is
vital, therefore, not to confuse increased provision with improved
provision. The latter may require the former, but the former does not
necessarily lead to the latter. (I particularly stress Cantor's remark,
'...although there is some evidence of a correlation between increased
and improved provision of education and training on the one hand and
greater productivity and a better economic performance on the other, it
is by no means crystal clear.

There is a second methodological point that needs to be taken
seriously. It can best be illustrated by examining chapter 5 by Prais,
although it has broader significance than that. It concerns the comparison with West Germany. Certain key differences from Britain are stated
relating to apprenticeships, vocational training in and out of school,
mathematical achievement and selection and the structure of the
secondary education system. They are not chosen arbitrarily, but are
meant to be important, especially in explaining differences in economic
performance. They are presented as relevant in the sense that lessons
can be learned from them, and British policy adapted accordingly.

Now, the comment I wish to make is not that Prais is mistaken. Quite the contrary, as he himself notes, it has been obvious for years that an educational system not geared explicitly and directly to the needs of the economy and especially the manufacturing sector will only yield economic benefits as a by-product, if at all. My question is simply, why these comparisons and no other? Should we not also emphasise such differences as the public schools (and the recruitment of their pupils by the City of London), the influence of Oxford and Cambridge generally, and the distorting role of all universities on school examinations? Are not the deeper questions: Why is British education altogether so anti-vocational, except for some professions? and Why does it still perpetuate the old fallacy of 'character moulding'?

Thus, following Prais, I would change the secondary curriculum. But it would be necessary to go altogether further if the objective was to bring United Kingdom economic performance up to the average of the advanced industrialised world. The objective would be a far ranging reform from the top down rather than from the bottom up. Moreover, I remain pessimistic about the possibility of actually destroying the deadening influence of the public schools, Oxford and Cambridge, and the City of London. To reiterate his point, the necessary action has been obvious for decades.

Given that, the chapters by Prais, Jones and Cantor lead us to consider the following questions:

(i) Is it desirable to organise post-compulsory education to a greater extent on a part-time basis? Should this be viewed as day-release from school, or day-release from work? In other words, what should the student regard as his home base?

(ii) How far does the system of grants, social security, and young person's wages need to be reformed to achieve a more desirable outcome? In this connection we need to examine the incentives given both to those who do the training and those who receive it? (Note chapter 4 on the structure of relative wages and chapter 3 on financial assistance for young people from poorer backgrounds.)

(iii) Suppose it can be established in the United Kingdom that too little training is offered both by schools and by industry. It would follow that, on average, training would have to be increased. Does it follow that the increase should be the same for all occupations and types of labour? (Note the reference in chapter 5 to retailing in Germany.)

(iv) If schooling for most people in the United Kingdom were moved in a more practical direction, would this necessarily be at the expense of education defined in its usual broad sense?

Concerning these questions I would draw two additional conclusions. One is that the responsibility in this field must be with central government. I would specially emphasise the need to keep the Department of Employment involved and not simply or even chiefly the Department of Education and Science. Above all I reject the view that the work of the Manpower Services Commission should be transferred to any great degree to the local authorities.

Secondly, if policy of the kind envisaged is to be successful (and also not hypocritical), aggregate demand must also be expanded to keep pace with aggregate supply and facilitate the return to full employment. Otherwise all that happens is that the employed and unemployed are shuffled around; one man's gain is another's loss.

Finally, I should like to add a couple of more technical comments on chapter 4.

It is an exceptionally good example of how important problems can be clarified using elementary analysis and empirical methods. I am extremely impressed with the way Jones emphasises the importance of the private costs and benefits as seen both by the employer and potential trainee. The two questions I would ask for the United Kingdom are as follows:

(i) If there is a large excess supply of trainees why do not more firms find ways of breaking the system of minimum wages? It would be profitable for them to do so, and those young people who would like to acquire skills, but are prevented from doing so, would gain too. Presumably, the institutional restraints are powerful, but are we not also observing the typical sluggishness of the United Kingdom labour market?

(ii) Essentially most of the data are the demand curves for trainees and for skilled labour. But an additional hypothesis concerns the determinants of those curves. In X-efficiency terms, are not British firms operating on lower production functions than are available? Do they not have a chronic tendency to undervalue skill (including above all on-line managerial skill)? Thus, is it not also an important research task to examine why the relevant demand curves are where they are?

In connection with (i) I am also led to query the assumption of the generality of skill that is acquired. While skills are transferable, they always have an element specific to the firm. If the cost of offering general skills is artificially high should there not be a tendency to substitute training in skills specific to the firm, and should not firms devote more energy to attracting workers to them? Does this actually happen more in the United Kingdom than abroad? Would it not also imply that there must be additional explanations of the differences in the extent of apprenticeship training?

All these relate to one final matter. Following the X-efficiency point, we are all now aware of how misleading is the economist's assumption of the given production function. Performance is determined more generally as part of the bargaining process. It is at least to some extent a choice variable under the partial control of both manager and worker. We must ask, therefore, why the skilled worker chooses and is allowed to choose as poor an operating level as he does? Here too, however, I recognise that all I am doing is finding work for Mr. Jones!

Comment on Chapters 3–5
by Sir Hugh Ford

The three papers in this session present an interesting analysis of the present position of the education and training of the 16–19 year age group. It is a sobering reflection that, despite all the analysis and self examination of the last twenty or even thirty years, we are still finding it necessary to go on analysing our education system. Surely so much analysis should by now have led to some actions of which at least some people approve? Yet the present authors are still saying that 'a fundamental re-thinking of our 'system' is necessary' or that there is little that is new in their conclusions from the analysis. It seems to me, therefore, that we are looking in the wrong place for the solution of our ills, and that it is an analysis of people that will be more useful.

We find ourselves in a world situation in which technology has demanded an extreme degree of specialisation in the provision of goods and services. The 'information technology' explosion will exacerbate this development, to the point where specialised interdependence and interaction become so critical that a breakdown of one cell in the vast complex will cause an immobilisation of the whole.

Against this background, a nation that does not recognise that it is immoral to withhold one's labour or service from one's fellow men to win a selfish advantage has little chance of long-term survival, let alone a betterment of its living standards. Couple with this the loss of our nineteenth century belief in the work ethos and there is, in my view, no difficulty in identifying where our real problem lies.

I submit it is in our attitude of mind that our malady lies, not in our educational system and until hard reality or a new inspiration forces us into a change of heart, we can analyse the shortcomings of this or that system of education and training to no purpose. It can be argued with some truth that the United Kingdom has for too long clung to the notion that 'education' rather than 'training' was the source from which a wise, disciplined and accomplished nation arose, and all subjects and techniques had to be made respectable by an academic and systematic process. Yet it has frequently been shown (and the armed forces are past masters at it) that a great many subjects – and not only at technical level – can be taught quickly and effectively when related to a specific application or to meet a particular need.

I served a five year apprenticeship in mechanical engineering ('fitting, turning and erecting') some fifty years ago. The incentive for doing so in my case was as a stepping stone to a career as a professional (that is Chartered) engineer, but for the average trade apprentice the incentives were the status that went with the skilled craftsman title and the significantly higher remuneration compared with the unskilled worker. The trades unions over the past fifty years have eroded both these incentives to the point where indentures are of little account and the young perceive themselves to be better off in highly paid, unskilled work.

This is the milieu in which the 16–19 age group finds itself. No changing of our system of education and training will have much effect unless the environment can inspire a new and positive attitude to skill and technique.

The need then, is to *do* something and to me the initiative of the present Government in launching the Youth Training Scheme (YTS) is admirable and to be encouraged and fostered by all means. While I found Cantor's paper a very valuable addition to our review, I reject the criticism that YTS had 'failed' because it had attracted 'only about 354,000' by March 1984 against a planned accommodation of about 460,000. To have achieved 354,000 entrants appears to me magnificent and a significant step towards a more technically competent young work force. The pressing need is for the courses to be directed towards the kinds of skill, knowledge and techniques to meet the widening gap in the new technologies. I believe there is no shortage of jobs – the shortage is of the right people with the right technical training to fill them.

Cantor's paper advocates a centralisation and control of all these endeavours. It seems to me that this will not only stifle initiatives but also add significantly to overhead costs at a time when budgets are limited and efficiency calls for the maximum resources being available at the working level.

Comment on Chapters 6 and 7
by Dermot Glynn

To put the descriptions in chapters 6 and 7 by d'Iribarne and Russell of the French and German systems into context, we should note that those who have attempted international comparisons of the training system have generally concluded that the United Kingdom compares unfavourably [1]. Although it may be impossible to prove a connection between training and economic performance, the dependence of performance on the skills and attitudes of the workforce at all levels is obvious enough; and so too is the influence for good or ill which can come from the system of education and training. We should also note that the new Youth Training Scheme (YTS) is being presented by the British Government in a very positive light, as a way of improving training and hence enhancing the economic outlook. It is widely believed that admiration for the German system in particular has influenced policy in the United Kingdom, and also in the EC more generally.

I wish to argue four main points: (i) that the case for more 'off-the-job' training in the United Kingdom is not as powerful as comparisons with Germany might suggest, (ii) that educationalists could well do more to study and disseminate the labour market 'signals' sent by employers; (iii) that the future of YTS will need more critical justification when youth unemployment is reduced; and (iv) that a significant contribution to achieving that would be to follow the German example and pay much lower rates to trainees.

The case for more 'off-the-job' training

Against this background, the question arises why training in Britain has apparently been so much less than elsewhere; and whether it is true that increased vocational training in schools, colleges or other 'off-the-job' situations will improve our economic performance. I would like to suggest some reasons for taking a cautious view on this.

Firstly, there is the matter of definitions. Implicit in many of these chapters is the view that training is a formal activity, carried out either in education establishments or during recognised special allocations of time with an employer. This at least allows some measurement; but it does not reflect the reality of continuing learning-by-doing which is a major feature of many jobs. Yet it is not at all clear why formal training should generally be superior to on-the-job learning, at least in terms of equipping the individual to perform well the tasks in question, and arguably in related positions to which he or she may subsequently move.

To include on-the-job, informal training in one's definition means that the difficulty of making international comparisons of the level or adequacy of vocational training is increased, but to the extent that this has not been done we should perhaps 'aim off' slightly from the impression given by comparisons of the time and money spent on formal training in different countries. The British youngster of 16 or 17 doing a job will very often be receiving some informal training and learning from experience; his (say German) counterpart in a training scheme may or may not be receiving more valuable formal training. Thus, the question of measuring the contribution of training to economic performance becomes even more complex than indicated in the main papers before the conference.

If the distinction between training and work is unclear, so too is that between training and education. I owe to Mr Roy Walker the thought that 'there is nothing quite so vocational as good A-levels in English, Maths and a well-chosen third subject'. Yet for practical purposes we do need to draw a distinction between education and training, if only because of the convention that the State should pay for education whilst employers should pay for (much of) the cost of training. (There is a familiar argument for training being financed by the state to some degree, to reflect the advantages to the individual and to other employers to whom a trained person may subsequently transfer).

With the YTS we are, however, currently moving away from the principle of the employer paying for training, and this raises the question why this should be so. My surmise is that this can be attributed to the political wish to prevent the worst manifestations of high youth unemployment, and to the willingness of Ministers to devote large amounts of government expenditure to this end. From that starting point, the options would effectively be to raise the school leaving age (which would not have been taken as a serious possibility in the present climate of opinion) or to find a combination of training and work experience.

Attributing some such political motive to the new policy does not mean that it is mistaken, but it does suggest that in developing future policy it would be sensible to try to leave as much as possible of the cost of training to be borne by employers at their discretion, whether this takes a formal or an informal on-the-job shape. The presumption that employers are the best judges of the type and amount of training required should not be set aside too easily.

Another reason for doubting whether economic performance would be improved by increased vocational training off the job is that this is not in general a priority for employers. Policy statements by individual employers and by the CBI show that United Kingdom employers are concerned about the values and personal qualities gained from the system of education and training, as well as about the particular skills learned. When considering how attributes of the workforce influence economic success, it would be wrong to focus mainly on the vocational skills taught by schools or colleges, or in formal training schemes. More important are flexibility, general abilities, and attitudes to work – all qualities developed during the years of education.

At this point we should note the contrast between the German and French models, and the Japanese. According to the results of a recent comparative study by Hayes and the IMS reported to the May 1984 meeting of the NEDC [2], the Japanese put their emphasis on education rather than training. 'Specialisation is avoided at all educational levels ..... emphasis is upon educating 'the whole person' (that is, including social skills) ..... general broad-based education is in harmony with the labour market. It provides the socialised, adaptable 'blank sheets' employers prefer .....'

There are some 'vocational' courses available to 15–18 year olds in the education system, but less than 30 per cent choose these, and the vocational content of the courses is less than 30 per cent. Thus effectively Japanese training begins with employment. Moreover, although major firms provide formal training, and expect employees to study also in their own time, the main emphasis appears to be on informal, on-the-job training (including the famous quality circles, and so on) the extent of which, although felt to be impressive, is not measured nor officially estimated.

As the cultural differences between the United Kingdom and Japan are even greater than between the United Kingdom and West Germany, the latter might be thought a better source of transferable ideas and methods. On the other hand, the Japanese economic success has been very great indeed; and the United Kingdom employers' representatives have, as noted above, tended to stress the need for sound general education and personal qualities rather than for specific vocational skills in those recruited from schools and other education. Moreover, the American system also appears to rely more than the German on learning by doing, or training by employers following a general education.

Nor are these the only reasons for suspecting that increased emphasis on general education as opposed to vocational training off the job might be better for future economic performance. If it is true that the development of new technologies will change the skills required in very many jobs, and also require people to adapt to new work in the course of their working lives, the broader educational base might well prove best. At least, the need for future flexibility is a good reason to avoid specialising too soon in specific vocational skills.

Labour market 'signals' – the requirements of employers
Recent Ministerial statements show a natural preference for increasing the influence on educational policy of labour market signals, and some impatience with a perceived failure of employers to make their requirements clearer. It appears that in Germany (for example) employers are given a great deal of influence over the educational and training system, which they exercise through well-organised local Chambers of Commerce. A connected criticism is that United Kingdom employers do not distinguish enough in their recruitment policies between (say) engineers – regarded by many as obviously essential for future economic success – and (say) generalists. Is this view reasonable? If employers do not offer more attractive jobs to, for

example, engineers, this is presumably either because more engineers are not required, or because employers fail to understand their own interests.

Except in cases where restrictive practices of one sort or another are important, the numbers of jobs offered and the rates of pay are the best guide to employer's current requirements. There is a good deal of scope for communicating these more fully to those involved in allocating educational resources and deciding curricula, and also to students deciding on training/education options. For example, the new DES publication, 'Graduates and Jobs', discusses the factors influencing employment prospects for graduates, and includes a table showing the percentage of graduates in each of 27 subjects (men) and 22 subjects (women) in 1982 who became unemployed. This should be useful to young people deciding on their choice of degree, and also to teachers and career advisers.

Extending such information would be a practical step towards improving the efficiency with which employers' 'signals' to the world of education and training are received. The extensions could cover:
(1) earnings: the average (and higher and lower) earnings of each type of graduate, by subject and by class of degree;
(2) other qualifications than degrees: the percentages of students entering the labour market with other qualifications who find employment, again showing the influence of the subjects studied and grades achieved, and earnings;
(3) colleges or other educational institutions: comparisons of the success of former students in the labour market.

Plainly, the last of these suggestions would be resisted by institutions fearing that the comparisons would put them in an unfavourable light; but it would be useful guidance for potential students and teachers.

It might be possible to draw together for the benefit of students and careers advisers the available research into the current recruiting policies and practices of employers; and perhaps the DES should encourage more colleges and schools to analyse the experience in the labour market of their own recent students.

In addition to improving in these and other ways the awareness by educationalists of current labour market signals, it should be worthwhile to encourage more formal consultation between educationalists and employers at local level. Such discussions could cover the development of curricula, and take account of changes expected in future employers' requirements and recruitment policies. These discussions should systematically cover the likely needs of small and new enterprises; and of sectors (such as some service industries) unlikely to be fully involved in any formal consultation.

Public expenditure
It is hard in present circumstances to feel critical of even very substantial public expenditure aimed at improving the prospects of school leavers. However, the view is sometimes advanced that money spent on retraining adults might have produced more economic advantage, for example, in helping to alleviate bottlenecks. It would be interesting to know to what extent the MSC has been able to analyse the costs and benefits of schemes designed to help different age groups.

On the broader level, if one accepts that in general reduced public expenditure assists economic development, should the spending on YTS be regarded as justified on economic or on social grounds? My impression is that it is accepted by employers primarily for the latter reason, shading into a long-term view of the economic disadvantage of large numbers of people who experienced long unemployment in their formative years, rather than as investment likely to produce economic benefit in the shorter term. This may not matter much in practice whilst youth unemployment remains unacceptably high; but in the longer term it will be important to know whether the cost – in public expenditure, to employers and to individuals – of the training given is justified in terms of increased economic contribution and earning power of the individuals concerned.

Pay rates for trainees
Perhaps the most striking of the 'lessons from abroad' before the conference are the comparisons in chapter 4 by Jones of rates of pay for trainees in the United Kingdom and Germany. There can be no doubt that the high cost to British employers of trainees is a factor limiting the numbers trained, both over the long run and in the recent sharp decline in the numbers of apprentices. These rates of pay have been sought by trade unions, partly in the perceived interests of older workers, and often conceded by employers as a relatively small item in the overall pay negotiation. If the lower rates in YTS, coupled with the German example, lead to a marked reduction in pay rates for trainees more generally, that would be a significant step towards improving the prospects for employment and training of young people.

References
[1] In addition to these chapters (6 and 7), see for example, speech by the Secretary of State for Employment, 4 May, 1984; 'Education for 16–19 year olds', report of Committee of Central and Local Government Experts chaired by Mr Macfarlane, December 1980

and 'Education for professional engineers and technologists', memorandum submitted to NEDC by the Secretary of State for Trade and Industry, February 1984.

[2] NEDC (84) 39, 'Education and training in Japan, the United States and West Germany'.

Comment on Chapters 5 and 6
by Roy Jackson

General

The chapters in this book suggest two issues for consideration – the school curriculum and the initial foundation training of young people. There is obviously a third – the training and retraining of adults. Indeed the lack of a system of industrial training and vocational education for adults is far more pronounced than for 14–19 year olds, but that must be for another discussion.

On the school curriculum and initial training the general tone of the chapters is pessimistic, notwithstanding the current crisis for educational finance. From a TUC perspective there has been considerable change in the views of major interests, and some encouraging developments over the last two decades. However, the present approach lacks an agreed strategy for coordinating the numerous initiatives that reflect a considerable consensus.

School curriculum

The TUC accepts that the effects (good or bad) of the influence of education on Britain's relatively poor economic performance are difficult to prove. Nevertheless we believe that public policy should encourage positive effects. The issue of balance in the curriculum is a major one, but HMI statements [1978, 1984] on the curriculum should provide us with an approach which is broadly acceptable to all. Any attempt to shape the school curriculum must be based on the needs of young people, as Gareth Williams has argued. There is some evidence in this book that the school curriculum is failing many young people who are under-achieving at school. The TUC would also support the view that such young people (as well as the more academically successful) can be motivated by the desire to fulfil themselves as adults. Also, these youngsters broadly accept the work ethic – even if such acceptance is coloured by criticism of economic failures in our society. Vocational studies/vocational preparation therefore can have some currency with young people, whereas the traditional 'academic' subjects – or subject teaching that ignores young people's basic motivations – can often fail.

As some authors argue, the school system (public examinations, the formation of teacher training and experience, the 'ivory tower' approach to curriculum issues and teaching methods) tends to isolate the school from adult life and industrial society.

Nevertheless the piecemeal approaches to curriculum change have been generated from within, as well as outside the system. For the TUC's part, we have been closely associated with the Schools Council Industry Project (SCIP). This is a good example of a 'bottom up' development, where teachers draw heavily on resources in the local industrial community.

The curriculum strategy used by SCIP involves linking schools with local industry – employers and trade unionists. Each participating local education authority (LEA) has to appoint a schools industry coordinator who works with the handful of schools involved. Backing up the coordinators is a small central team providing briefings and workshops for teachers and the employers and trade unionists supporting the different schools. The experience of SCIP illustrates the direction the curriculum needs to take if it is to develop a useful relationship with industry.

Rather than teachers handing out chunks of predigested knowledge, schools involved in SCIP have tried out new ways of working. For example, classroom studies have been linked with work experience – where pupils get a first-hand impression of what it is like to be at work, how workplaces operate, and how the functions of different people in the workplace interrelate. This experience is brought back to the classroom. In another interesting development, schools invite trade unionists and employers to give advice on the content of courses and to help teachers in practical classroom work, using case studies and role-playing exercises.

So far a third of LEAs are involved in SCIP but only a handful of schools. At the present rate of development (it started in 1978), it will take decades to involve all schools.

The MSC's Technical and Vocationed Education Initiative (TVEI) has a similar approach. It too has clear national criteria but the LEA is responsible for deciding the instruments it will use for accommodating them. The TVEI pilot projects have to link into existing examination and certificated courses and specifically provide resources for in-service teacher training. But the examination requirements are laid down by the examining body – and that could be a straight-jacket.

There is reason to believe that it will not be long before all or most LEAs are involved in the TVEI. But the resource implications of moving from the handful of schools/colleges involved in each LEA to make comprehesive provision for all schools and colleges are very considerable and as yet the political will is not there to deliver the resources.

The Secretary of State for Education and Science, however, is now adopting a more strategic approach to curriculum change. Curriculum objectives are to be defined for each subject area, and the examination system is to be changed from a norm-referenced one to one based on criterion referencing. Examination reform will be the Trojan Horse. Examinations will have a more direct influence over the detail of what is taught in classrooms. Criteria referencing will require new grade-related criteria – so there will be much closer definition of what you actually need to learn and achieve to gain a certain grade. The intention is to enable 80-90 per cent of young people to attain higher examination passes. However the effect could be to allow the examining boards to dictate the curriculum. Are we in danger of consolidating fragmented subject teaching, rather than breaking down rigid subject boundaries? Above all, would defined curricular objectives be based on teachers' experience, and would the exercise still allow teachers to be responsive to differing needs and circumstances and to innovate? How would other interests (including employers and trade unions) contribute? The last thing we want is a more rigid, centrally controlled curriculum.

The way the Secretary of State chooses to proceed will be decisive. Examination reform must be curriculum led; curriculum change must be based on sound processes of testing and piloting change by teachers themselves; all change must be supported through appropriate teacher training and other services. Those three inputs: curriculum development, examination reform and teacher training need to be coordinated at national level, possibly through a new national representative body, backed up by adequate resources.

Initial foundation training of young people
The papers reveal the main problems hindering policy development in this area: the past failure to provide opportunities for the majority of young people and the gross failure to deliver equal opportunities for girls; the current collapse of the apprenticeship system; the ineffectiveness of narrow job-specific training, given the pace of technological change; the disincentives for young people to follow education-based vocational provision; the difficulties in establishing YTS as a credible permanent training scheme and failure to provide for *all* young people seeking to enter the labour market; and the lack of cohesion across training and education for young people with increased friction in the education/MSC interface.

The recent developments upon which a 'system' could be built do, however, need recognition. In education there is the MSC Technical and Vocational Education Initiative. Apart from introducing technical education into the fourth and fifth years of secondary education it will enable young people to acquire a technical or vocational qualification. Additionally there is the new, as yet untested, one-year course based on the Certificate of Pre-Vocational Education. These two initiatives could provide a wide range of both specific and broad-based vocational preparation and are in addition to the specific courses provided by the Business Education Council/Technical Education Council (BEC/TEC). The possibility clearly exists of establishing a comprehensive framework of full-time and part-time education-based vocational courses for young people offering a wide variety of occupational choices.

The YTS can similarly develop into a permanent scheme of foundation training meeting the initial needs of all school-leavers. The achievement to date has been the provision of an adequate stock of places and the establishment of a structure at national and local levels: the Youth Training Board; Advisory Group for Content and Standards; Accredited Training Centres; and Area Manpower Boards. But the difficulties that remain are considerable. Given the workplace base of most YTS schemes there are serious doubts about the ability of employers and others to meet the training criteria and broader educational objectives; likewise there is a lack of understanding by supervisors about relating job skills, specific to their workplace, to other related occupations (occupational training families); there are problems in integrating work experience with the off-the-job education and training; there is the need to establish effective monitoring and development procedures *within each scheme* (programme review teams) as well as to establish effective public accountability; and there is a need to involve young people. All these issues are in play within the MSC structures. A key issue is the training of trainers and supervisors for which very few resources are available.

The need is to ensure that the system of education and training for 16-19 year olds offers all young people a varied choice of provision that caters for personal development and future careers. The present arrangement falls far short of this. A strategy might need to include the following elements: (a) mandatory education maintenance allowances for those opting for full-time education-based provision; (b) coordination of content/curriculum course entry requirements and so on, to ensure that individual progression is encouraged; for example, YTS to longer-term training or return to full-time study; and for facilitating some switching of young people between different courses/provisions; (c) coordination needs to reflect LEAs (colleges of FE), examining bodies (BTEC, CGLI), Further Education Units and MSC along with DES and Department of Employment. Already much cross-fertilisation between these bodies exists but some means of agreeing a broad approach and a 'clearing house' to ensure coordination is needed. A Department of Education/Training is *not* an answer. Such a Department would still have to control LEAs - which is not desirable. It also ignores the powerful case for linking training to employment - the role of Department of Employment and MSC; (d) the need to ensure *all* employers provide for the initial foundation training of young people. This will almost certainly involve placing some statutory duty on employers to train to the standards of YTS. Employers would still have choice whether to join YTS, and young people would have a whole range of options still open to them at 16.

Summary of the Discussion

The Conference considered the implications for relative economic performance of the large disparity in trained persons between Britain and Germany revealed in Prais's work. It was noted that the data related only to the outcomes of formal training provision and therefore did not cover the large amount of informal off-the-job training that must occur in any economy; that any conclusion drawn from a two-country comparison must inevitably be highly tentative; and that no systematic evidence had been offered to link British deficiencies in training to economic performance. Evidence of the effects of the British deficiencies in both intermediate and high-level skills was, however, beginning to emerge from studies of matched British and German manufacturing plants. These suggested that because of their relative deficiency in shop floor skills, equivalent British plants had to carry more overhead labour in the form of quality controllers, production planners, and so on, and that the comparative shortage of maintenance skills in British plants might be associated with longer equipment down-time and hence lower capital productivity.

Attention was drawn to the contrasts in the pattern of training provision between Germany and Japan, another highly successful economy. Japan appeared to be following a policy of *reducing* the vocational content of general schooling, which was now almost universal up to the age of 18. Specific occupational training was being increasingly concentrated in the early years of employment at 18-plus. The German 'dual system' emphasises vocational training with a limited general educational content for a large proportion of the 15-18 age group. Was there perhaps a danger that the German system might prove less adaptable than the Japanese in the face of rapid technical change? The syllabuses used in certain training occupations in Germany appeared in the past to have remained unchanged for many years. Against this, it was suggested that the formal syllabuses in Germany were concerned with minimum standards and that the overall content of training was responsive to the needs of technical change. Also, the German system was concerned with the appreciation of the need to maintain high standards in work of all kinds as well as with the attainment of technical competence in the chosen training occupation. 'Intangible' effects of this kind would clearly need to be considered in any assessment of the economic significance of the over-training which appears to occur in certain training occupations in Germany.

As to the source of the British deficiency in formal vocational training, some participants were inclined to emphasise the role of market failure on the side of employers' demand for trainees arising from the fear of poaching, rather than excessively high trainee wages. A free market, it was argued, would not deliver a socially optimal quantity or quality of training and what was needed was either some form of levy-grant or remissable tax arrangement. But no clear or convincing explanation was forthcoming as to why the training market had apparently failed to a much greater extent in Britain than in other countries with workplace-based training systems. Others pointed to the absence of a strong tradition of systematic labour force training in Britain; what was needed, in this area, was for the MSC vigorously to go out and sell the 'training idea' to employers.

The increase in trainee pay in Britain to its current relatively high levels appears to have been the outcome of trade union pressure in the 1930s. This occurred in response to the decreasing effectiveness of the journeyman–apprentice ratio as a means of regulating entry into the skilled trades in the face of pressure from employers. However, once established, the situation may have been rationalised in terms of the 'worth' of apprentices vis-à-vis other young people and this may explain its persistence through the postwar period even in the face of radically changed labour market conditions.

Further evidence of the rigidities of the British labour market was to be found in the observation that adult skill differentials in Britain appeared to be similar to those in Germany and Switzerland despite the relative shortage of skills in Britain. Individuals also appeared to be more prepared to invest in themselves through further vocational training as adults in the United States, Germany and Japan than in Britain. Once again, this might reflect the suppression of pay differentials within the British system of collective bargaining.

Finally, it was noted that the history of warnings about the inadequacy of British vocational training stretched back to before 1914. Why, as in the field of education generally, had not clearly perceived needs found expression in official policy-making?

Part 3   Education

8   The Bottom Half in Lower Secondary Schooling
by T. Neville Postlethwaite

Prais [3] compared the 1964 mathematics achievement of West German and English Form 3 pupils. This chapter presents such evidence as is available about standards of achievement in several industrialised countries including West Germany and England. The only available data are those from the International Association for the Evaluation of Educational Achievement (IEA). The first set of data to be presented is from the IEA science and reading comprehension surveys conducted in 1970. The goodness of sampling and the validity of the tests have been described elsewhere [1,2 and 4].

The second set of data is from the IEA mathematics study conducted in 1981. The goodness of sampling and the validity of tests for this second mathematics study have not yet been published but would appear to be in order for the population results presented here.

It seems appropriate to examine pupils' achievement towards the end of compulsory schooling when the whole of an age group is in school. For science and reading comprehension the population group for which data are available includes all pupils aged 14.0–14.11 on the day of testing. For the second mathematics study it was all pupils in the modal grade for 13 year olds. For the purpose of comparison, I have selected Scotland, Sweden, United States, Hungary and Japan to compare with England.

Dispersion of scores
One measure of the dispersion of scores is the standard deviation. The means and standard deviations for the total population (14 year olds) are given for science and reading comprehension in table 8.1.

With the exception of Japan for science, England consistently has the largest standard deviation. What we do not know is how the distribution is made up. Are there, for example, certain school types with very high scores and others with very low ones? No national analyses were undertaken on the English data to yield such information. Such information could still be produced but, given the dramatic shift to comprehensive schools in England, it is doubtful if it

Table 8.1   Means, standard deviation and N's for 14 year olds in science and reading comprehension, 1970

	Science			Reading Comprehension		
	$\overline{X}$	SD	N	$\overline{X}$	SD	N
England	21.3	14.1	3090	25.3	11.9	3087
Scotland	21.4	14.2	1980	27.0	11.5	1964
Sweden	21.7	11.7	2328	25.6	10.8	2281
US	21.6	11.6	4194	27.3	11.6	3503
Hungary	29.1	12.7	6942	25.5	9.8	6950
Japan	31.2	14.8	1946	—	—	—

Source: International Association for the Evaluation of Educational Achievement.

Chart 8.1   The distribution of the bottom half of scores in science in selected countries, 1970

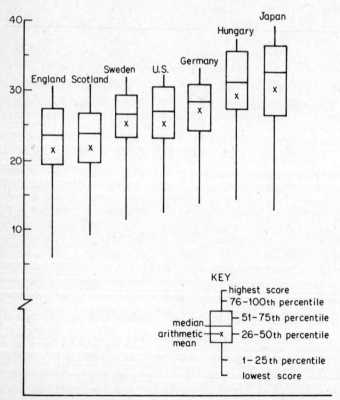

Source: See table 8.1

would be useful today, although it might be of historical interest. And the move to comprehensive-type schools, it must be remembered, was much more on socio-political grounds than on educational grounds.

The bottom half for science and reading comprehension

Prais has pointed to the problem of adequacy of schooling for those going from school to work at the end of compulsory schooling. Given that it is different proportions of an age group which go from school to work, or school to apprenticeship to work, in different countries, charts 8.1 and 8.2 compare the bottom 50 per cent of a distribution of achievement in several countries on the assumption that it is that group which tends to enter work immediately after the end of compulsory schooling.

Chart 8.2   The distribution of the bottom half of scores in reading comprehension in selected countries

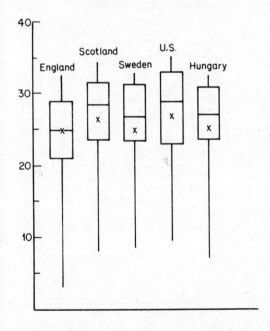

Key: See chart 8.1.
Source: See table 8.1

England's bottom 50 per cent perform at a lower level than the other countries' bottom 50 per cents with which comparisons are made – even lower than the United States. The German–Swedish comparison is of interest in the science results. Germany in 1970 had primarily a selective school system with *Hauptschule*, *Realschule* and *Gymnasium* at the 14 year old level. Sweden, by 1968, had only comprehensive schools.

Chart 8.3 presents the results of preliminary analysis undertaken on the data from the 1981 IEA second mathematics study. England ranks second lowest for the bottom half of the distribution.

Chart 8.3   Full distributions in mathematics (1981) for England and other selected countries [a]

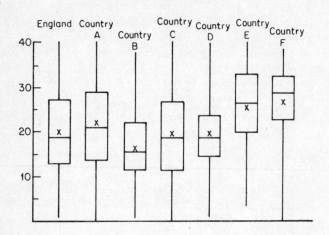

Key: See chart 8.1.

Note: [a] The data used were those on the cleaned files in the IEA data processing center in New Zealand. The student N in the English data set was 3206. The bottom 50 per cent, therefore, consists of 1803 students. Because of IEA release of data rules, it is not possible to identify the other countries which are presented in chart 8.3 and table 8.2. However, they are not too different from the countries presented in chart 8.1. The identification of the countries is not too important – the important feature is how England's bottom 50 per cent compares with the bottom 50 per cent in some other industrial countries. Permission to identify England in these preliminary analyses has been granted by the National Foundation for Educational Research in England and Wales.

The results presented in chart 8.3 are based on the so-called core test only – a test taken by all children. The test had 40 items covering those aspects of mathematics judged to be important in all participating countries. There were other tests which were rotated over all children such that a quarter of the children took each test. From the totality of tests it was possible to derive certain sub-scores in mathematics. These are presented in table 8.2 for the total distribution of children. It would be possible to calculate the same sub-scores for the bottom 50 per cent of children but this has not yet been done.

Table 8.2   Means and standard deviations $^{\underline{a}}$ of mathematics sub scores

Full distribution	England	Country B	Country D	Country E	Country F
Arithmetic					
total (46)	22.16	18.69	26.51	26.10	27.73
	(5.60)	(5.74)	(3.35)	(5.66)	(2.89)
computation (17)	8.56	7.49	11.67	10.71	11.70
	(2.20)	(2.33)	(1.27)	(2.20)	(1.20)
higher level (29)	13.61	11.19	14.86	15.37	16.02
	(3.63)	(3.52)	(2.28)	(3.64)	(1.84)
Algebra					
total (30)	12.01	9.68	16.49	15.11	18.08
	(3.76)	(3.09)	(3.06)	(4.04)	(2.12)
computation (14)	5.64	4.27	8.45	7.24	9.09
	(1.94)	(1.61)	(1.51)	(2.03)	(1.17)
higher level (16)	6.35	5.39	8.01	7.86	8.99
	(1.99)	(1.65)	(1.71)	(2.16)	(1.11)
Geometry					
total (39)	17.47	15.37	14.80	20.84	22.43
	(4.31)	(3.99)	(2.74)	(4.59)	(2.13)
Plane G (19)	9.32	8.40	8.17	11.83	12.61
	(2.26)	(2.32)	(1.57)	(2.34)	(1.16)
Transformation G (8)	3.85	3.29	2.99	4.57	4.76
	(1.08)	(0.92)	(0.65)	(1.24)	(0.63)
Whole numbers (10)	5.88	4.87	6.94	6.77	6.88
	(1.09)	(1.48)	(0.81)	(0.98)	(0.75)
Proportional thinking (14)	7.07	6.02	6.77	8.14	8.80
	(1.70)	(1.87)	(1.27)	(1.82)	(1.06)
Statistics (18)	10.83	10.14	10.33	10.86	12.75
	(1.90)	(2.74)	(1.51)	(2.00)	(1.07)
Standard Units of Measurement (5)	2.84	3.72	4.38	4.21	3.94
	(0.60)	(0.72)	(0.25)	(0.41)	(0.31)
Measurement (24)	11.66	11.69	14.27	14.90	16.47
	(2.82)	(3.35)	(1.45)	(2.45)	(1.44)
Estimation and Approximation (12)	6.53	6.76	8.03	7.96	8.31
	(1.45)	(1.93)	(0.75)	(1.23)	(0.74)
Equations and inequations (8)	3.15	2.43	4.28	3.60	4.61
	(1.10)	(0.84)	(0.91)	(1.12)	(0.62)

$^{\underline{a}}$ In brackets below mean.

See also note to chart 8.3.

The number of items for each sub-test are given in parentheses after the name of the sub-test in column 1. In table 8.2 all scores are weighted but in chart 8.3 the scores are unweighted. However, in table 8.2, the general picture is clear and even for total distributions, England does not come too well out of the comparisons.

Possible causes and remedies
From the evidence above it is clear that in England for all Form 3 pupils

and, in particular, the bottom half of students, the level of achievement is poor. Why this might be, and what might be done about it, brings us into the realms of speculation. In this section I set down some of my own ideas about remedies. They cannot be inferred from the data presented in the first section. This would require between-country multivariate analyses which are not possible given the limited number of countries. Rather, they represent the thoughts of a researcher who has been involved in research and development in various countries with the aim of improving cognitive achievement.

Before beginning to speculate it should be mentioned that education is a tricky subject to write about since it tends often to generate emotional defensive reactions rather than rational ones. It is, of course, always possible to talk of stress or suicides in other systems of education (often based on highly misleading media reports) or, it is possible to argue that such and such a theme which is important in England has been given relatively little emphasis in the test. However, in the IEA tests, each participating research centre had a national subject area committee which undertook the various content analyses needed to produce a grid of objectives reflecting what was meant to have been learned by the end of Form 3. Suffice it to say at this point, that although there may be quibbles on matters of detail, the final tests may be judged reasonably valid for all countries.

Finally, the interpretation of the data and speculation are all a matter of the testimony, memory and introspection of the interpreter or speculator.

From another study which IEA conducted, the Classroom Environment Study, which examined teacher instructional and managerial behaviour associated with growth in achievement (after holding beginning of year performance and home background constant), it was clear that the following factors were important: (a) time on task; (b) quick disciplining of pupils, when necessary; (c) teachers being perceived by pupils to have high standards and demand a lot; (d) teachers getting feedback from children as to what they don't know or what problems they are having and doing something about it; (e) teachers being perceived to help children in terms of distinguishing important from less important aims and tasks; (f) frequent use of relevant examples over and above what is in the textbook. To burlesque the results, teachers should work hard, work the children hard and be quick on discipline.

To what extent do schools mirror society? Have traditional values, such as hard work and pride in professionalism, deteriorated in English society? Do many teachers now regard teaching as a 9 to 4 job rather than helping each child (even after school hours) to get as far as he or she can? Does the curriculum not demand too little from pupils? Japan, for example, demands quite a bit more of its pupils in science than other countries. Who determines the curriculum in England? On what basis? Have good 'needs assessment' studies been conducted to identify what the changing economic demands (changing demands of jobs) are/will be? If such studies have been conducted, are the results fed to the curriculum developers?

Examinations can be a motivating force for pupils to learn if two conditions can be fulfilled. The first is that the pupils see the relevance of the substance to be learned in terms of their own condition, a point to be dealt with later, and the second is that examination results are seen to be useful for obtaining employment. It is also clear that there should be a one-to-one relationship of the examination to what was to have been learned.

In general, it should be possible to create a curriculum which is seen to be relevant and, therefore, hopefully intrinsically motivating. With high unemployment in England, there must be some doubt about the second condition being fulfilled. On the other hand, it can always be argued that, in a time of job scarcity, those with better qualifications are more likely to succeed in obtaining employment than those with poorer qualifications – an argument that teachers surely use!

A point that is sometimes made is that education, as at present structured, involves pupils envisaging long-term goals: an examination at 15, then an apprenticeship and finally a 'proper' job. Some children (the bottom 20 per cent?) are, for whatever reason, incapable of thinking in terms of long-term goals, At best, they require a series of short-term goals. If this is true, what sorts of reform could be introduced (after appropriate innovation and evaluation) to ameliorate the plight of such pupils?

At this point I would suggest the following, somewhat naively perhaps, and somewhat peremptorily in order to stimulate discussion: (a) create a good national curriculum development centre specifically for core subjects (that is, English, mathematics, science, social studies) for the secondary education forms up to the end of compulsory education. The centre should produce one national curriculum or alternative curricula and should not only produce textbooks but also formative tests and remedial materials. The revision of the curriculum must work on a cyclical basis.

(b) Introduce compulsory in-service training for teachers for new content, strategies and methods.

(c) Create one national examination body linked to the curriculum centre for the core subjects. A series of sequenced examinations could be produced. Using Mode C of examining, class work could be involved in a form of continous assessment or particular themes in certain schools could be examined where it is thought that regional variation in core subjects might be called for. The sequencing could allow examinations at lower levels than Form 4.

If the curriculum is relevant, if it stretches pupils, if teachers know how to have feedback from every pupil on which specific learning objectives they have achieved and are well prepared to know what to do to ensure that all, or nearly all, pupils achieve each objective, then there is hope.

References

[1] Comber, L.C. and Keeves, John P., *Science Education in Nineteen Countries: An Empirical Study*, International Studies in Evalution, Vol. I., Stockholm: Almqvist & Wiksell; and New York, John Wiley & Sons, 1973.

[2] Peaker, Gilbert F., *An Empirical Study of Education in Twenty One Countries: A Technical Report*, International Studies in Evaluation, Vol. VIII, New York, John Wiley & Sons, 1975.

[3] Prais, S.J. and Wagner, K., Schooling standards in Britain and Germany: some summary comparisons bearing on economic efficiency, National Institute of Economic and Social Research, Discussion paper no. 14, 1983.

[4] Thorndike, Robert L., *Reading Comprehension in Fifteen Countries: An Empirical Study*, International Studies in Evaluation, Vol. III, Stockholm, Almqvist & Wiksell; and New York, John Wiley & Sons, 1973.

9 Productivity and Educational Values
by William Taylor

The story is told of a Scottish clergyman disturbed in the middle of the night by a furious knocking on his door. Opening it, he found himself confronted by one of his parishioners, obviously the worse for wear, who burst out, 'I must talk to ye, for I canna' sleep for thoughts of the awfu' schisms in the Kirk o' God'. 'Now then, Sandy', replied the Minister, 'you go on home and come back at 4 o'clock tomorrow afternoon when you're sober and then we can talk about the awful schisms in the Kirk of God'. 'Och, but tha's nae guid', replied the parishioner, 'for when I'm sober I dinna care a hoot about the awfu' schisms in the Kirk o' God.

Periodically, policy-makers and the public find themselves sleepless in the face of the economic and social problems facing the country. They turn to educators for a view on the part that schooling has played in bringing about the present state of affairs and what might now be done to improve matters. They soon find that the educators cannot come up with politically convincing answers; there appears to be no educational 'fix'. Worse, some of them start to query the assumptions that underlie the questioning. Are education and training compatible? Education has been defined as initiation into a worthwhile form of life. What if the work experience of most people is not worthwhile in this sense, if it debases and demoralises rather than challenges and satisfies? Why should schools be responsive to social change that dehumanises and limits opportunities for the full expression of human potentiality? What does it mean to know about industry? Is this to be the result of disinterested study, or of an attempt to socialise students to industrial values? And so on in like vein. Irritated, the enquirers return to their easier to quantify supply-side factors, such as capital stocks and the effects of multi-union industrial organisations on overmanning. Yet the concerns remain. If the British do not put such high priority on economic success – either personal or national – as do some of their competitors, then surely schools, colleges and universities have had something to do with this, reflecting, fostering, reinforcing, even perhaps creating particular attitudes and social values relevant to our relatively poor economic performances? [1,9].

Nineteenth century success – and failure
Historians who tackle these questions have to decide how far back to

go. Is the often remarked individualism of the British part of the answer? Do we then have to examine the social and economic conditions of the twelfth or thirteenth centuries to discover its origins? Fortunately most students of the subject adopt a shorter time perspective. Attention focuses on the late nineteenth century. Between 1850 and 1900, it is argued, a second industrial revolution occurred. Competitive success came to depend upon the existence of a stronger scientific and research base, on the availability of literate men and scientifically competent managers. Due to features of our social structure, and associated failures in educational reform, these requirements could not be met. We were late in reforming secondary education, late in developing scientific curricula, late in recognising the dangers of the waste of talent from insufficient access to education for able working-class children. Self-made men sent their sons to public schools and the ancient universities. There they acquired, not skills and knowledge to improve the family business, but social credentials for membership of a ruling class, a class that had its roots in the hereditary principle and the ownership of land. Trade and commerce it despised.

This thesis is now well documented [24,25]. Numerous studies show our lack of literacy, our high proportion of untrained managers, the difficulties that outsiders had in obtaining employment at any level in industries where apprenticeship was the rule and fathers expected there to be a place for their sons (an expectation not entirely absent from the rhetoric of contemporary industrial disputes).

Industrialisation and culture
During the past five years students of British cultural history have offered new insights on the development of some of our contemporary educational assumptions. Martin Wiener [28] argues that traditional mercantile and agrarian values, unbroken by revolutions of the kind that convulsed other countries, successfully resisted emergent industrial values and continued to dominate educational provision. Heyck [13] suggests that the great developments in academic science in the second half of the nineteenth century encouraged a high valuation of disciplinary specialisation, contrary to the early Victorian premium on synthesis. The scientist, a title to which students of history, of education and of many other emerging disciplines aspired, achieved status not by proposing new syntheses or identifying practical applications, but by making a contribution to advancing a specialism [13, p.81].

There was also the impact on Victorian consciousness of the deplorable social conditions of nineteenth century industrial Britain. The writings of Ruskin, of Morris, and their anti-bourgeois, romantically inspired interpreters, suggested that more humane, person-centred, community-based values needed to supplant the emptiness of material acquisition. There was a certain vagueness about how this might come about. Writers in this tradition are customarily short on the practicalities of social action and its implications. (But not always; see Inglis [14] on William Morris, for example.) Whatever the merits of their ideas, they inevitably cast doubt on the importance of values associated with production and with trade and commerce. Yet, although radical, even sometimes socialist, in inspiration and presentation, many of the images of this movement were just as much rooted in the pastoral tradition and a sense of lost community as those of the traditional aristocracy. In effect, if not in intention, they were reactionary, sharing the same contempt for industrial progress and material standards as some critics today accuse the ecological movement of encouraging.

There was a significant Christian input to this tradition of social criticism. Cowling ([18], p.xii) has argued that it 'is from religion that modern English intellectual history should begin' and that, 'the academic university is a fragment from a larger culture in which learning was inseparable from religion'. It is easy for those whose focus is on social differences to forget that much of the public argument about education in the late nineteenth century was not between classes, but between state and church. There were plenty of thoughtful churchmen who saw and spoke out against the moral debasement that industrialisation entailed, not only for its victims, but also for those who profited from its successes.

We must be careful about making too clear an identification between prominent nineteenth century social critics and the anti-industrial values that, it has been argued, characterise important areas of educational theory and practice today. Ruskin has been much quoted in this context, especially his impact upon the early development of the British Labour Party. Barker [3] refers to the survey that W. T. Stead, editor of the *Review of Reviews*, conducted in 1906 among all Labour and Lib-Lab MPs, to ascertain which books had most influenced them. Marx was mentioned twice. So was Plato. The Bible received fourteen mentions, Carlyle thirteen, John Stuart Mill ten – and Ruskin sixteen. In Ramsay MacDonald's words: '... the growth of the Labour Party has been owing to the rise within Labour organisations of an intellectual class of workmen who were influenced a good generation later than the intellectual classes were by the literacy and spiritual movements of the Mid-Victorian time embodied in the works of Carlyle and Ruskin' ([3], p.5).

Vocationalism and educational opportunity

For many readers the works of Ruskin codified or strengthened a dislike for the social and moral consequences of industrialisation that readily extended to the whole realm of money and trade. But if he was by no means always clear or consistent in his economic reasoning, a simple contempt for business was not one of Ruskin's central tenets. On the contrary. As Anthony ([12], p.36) has recently pointed out, his concern was with its remoralisation, with the 'infusion of moral responsibility into what have become self-interested and calculating relationships'.

Succeeding generations of socialist thinkers and writers were less concerned about cultural debasement and philistinism than lack of educational opportunity and occupational mobility. They were more familiar with Marx, ready to look for economic causes and political remedies for the condition of the working classes. They showed little interest in the problems of production and the threat of international competition to which Huxley had drawn attention in the mid-nineteenth century.

Saved from the sharp shocks of political and social revolution that afflicted many other countries, British society took longer to work out reforms to bring its social and educational arrangements into line with what was needed to consolidate and build upon the advantages conferred by its early start. In this context, it was difficult for any proposal to be examined on its merits that had to do with the provision of technical education, or with securing greater 'vocational relevance', or with giving young people educational experiences that would fit them for the kinds of lives they were likely to lead after leaving school. In the political context of the first half of the twentieth century, such proposals were judged according to whether they would limit or extend opportunities for boys and girls from working- and middle-class backgrounds to compete on equal terms with their better placed contemporaries. The curriculum, organisation and values of local authority secondary schools set up after 1902 represented no radical departure with late nineteenth century concepts of what secondary education should be about. They were sharply distinguished, however, from Technical Institutes and classes 'which devote themselves mainly to giving specialised instruction and training in certain subjects to young persons and adults who should previously have completed a sound general education...' [6].

By the 1920s, many Conservatives were convinced that something had to be done to reduce the waste of talent that arose from the elementary schools being, in the words of the President of the Board of Education, Eustace Percy, 'as much finishing schools for manual workers as Miss Pinkerton's academy was a finishing school for young ladies; and a class education of this kind was coming to be increasingly suspected and resented' [20]. On the left, there was growing sensitivity to the issue of access to secondary education. Yet, as Barker ([3], p.54) had pointed out, 'The parties shared a common assumption that secondary (grammar) education was a prize for the few; for Labour, Conservative and Liberals agreed in regarding the grammar school as an elite institution .... The argument was about access to educational privilege...'

In this context, any appeal for greater relevance, any untoward stress on training as distinct from education, ran the risk of being seen to serve other than educational purposes. It was one thing for Tawney to say that there was no question of imposing secondary education of the existing kind on all children. It was quite another to evolve politically acceptable alternatives consistent with English social and cultural circumstances.

Such international comparisons as featured in the educational thinking of the time had more to do with politics and foreign affairs than with industry and trade. One of my predecessors at the London Institute, Sir Percy Nunn, wrote in 1937: '... the traditional school needs to be radically altered if we desire a new sort of world. There must be less competition and more co-operation of the sort not directed against others. There must be greater informality and complete respect for the individuality of the pupil. In addition, there must be ample creative outlets for the stimulation and release of the imagination. There must be free speech and free thought. Above all, there must be a belief in the value of persuasion rather than of force. This involves as a corollary a willingness to put up with a certain amount of 'untidiness'. Only dictators can hope to have everything cut and dried, conforming constantly to a predetermined pattern' [18].

It is fashionable to be hard on such progressive sentiments. But as Stuart Maclure points out in chapter 10, educational discourse takes its colour from the priorities and concerns of its time. It was the rise of the dictators, not the condition of industry, that preoccupied many thoughtful people in the 1930s and which stimulated their identification with so-called progressive values. And for many, the ultimate triumph of the democracies in the ensuing war seemed to confirm the priority of 'free speech and free thought', creative imagination, and 'a certain amount of untidiness'. There were high hopes that the schools of the future would operate in a society very different from that of the past. This 1945 statement [11] by two experienced educational administrators was not untypical of its period: 'In the ideals of the new social order, profit making has no place. Drive and energy in all branches of industry, business and the professions must derive their motive power from the desire of all to promote the common good. This is the only incentive acceptable within the ideals of the new social order. In school we have to find motives for work and conduct appropriate to our times ... The teacher's usual stock-in-trade – the formal timetable, set schemes of work, syllabuses of instruction – will have to be adapted for new purposes, and, in the process, some of it may have to be scrapped.'

Productivity and politics in the postwar world

The British preoccupation with fairness has often been noted. When combined with the elements of cultural history already referred to, and with the realities of continuing social inequalities and unequal class chances in access to education, there is little difficulty in understanding why so much postwar educational discussion was – and to some extent remains – focused upon distribution rather than production, on how the cake of opportunity and status is to be shared out rather than on how it might be made bigger.

Britain's economic performance during the immediate postwar period was largely successful in fulfilling expectations conditioned by the assumptions and experience of the 1930s. The British public began to accustom itself to the idea of long-term affluence and a coming age of leisure.

Such optimism did not survive the reappearance of the same standard of comparison that Huxley had wanted to emphasise a hundred years before – not our own performance in the past, but that of other industrialised countries in the present. By the mid-1960s, academic and political concern was being expressed about our failures in productivity, in innovation and in trade. The response of the education system was affected by the active reassertion of anti-industrial, anti-growth values, derived partly from quality of life and moral debasement arguments of the kind earlier associated with Ruskin and Morris, and reinforced by concern with resource depletion and pollution. Scepticism about the benefits of continued economic growth and enhanced productivity has emanated from both right and left. A rampant capitalism has been no more popular with aristocrats than with collectivists. The views of those who saw (and sometimes sought) limits to growth gained support from the oil shocks of the 1970s and the recession that followed. It was not until after the middle of the decade that interest in what the education system might do to halt and to reverse the deterioration of our economic fortunes vis-à-vis our industrial competitors began to manifest itself. The Department of Education's Yellow Book [12]; James Callaghan's Ruskin College speech; the establishment of the Youth Opportunities Programme; a new press for greater accountability in education, with more emphasis on regular assessment and on the role of the inspectorate; the initiation of the CBI's Understanding British Industry project and the Royal Society of Arts' Education for Capability movement, were all indications of fresh attention being given to ways in which education related to economic performance.

The character of this attention, as of the scepticism of those who saw in it a threat to liberal educational values, had many familiar elements. Complaints about inadequate attainments of school-leavers and lack of relevance of school curricula to subsequent occupational requirements were as much in evidence as in earlier periods. So were fears about the dangers of reinforcing class divisions through differentiated programmes and the limitation of work experience to the academically less able. But on both sides there were elements that were new.

There was recognition, born of earlier manpower planning efforts and studies of industrial training needs, that improved economic performance was unlikely to come simply from trying to target teaching and training to specific labour force requirements. A prolonged period of specific cognitive and skills training is indispensable in many high level occupations. Nevertheless, even at graduate level the needs of most industrial and service employers are best met by a workforce with good 'trainability'. It has been argued that specific degree subjects are only strictly relevant in one case in three [22,23]. This is even more evident at other employment levels. Ill-considered vocational specificity in schooling can produce trained incapacity that reduces rather than enhances employability.

This not only emphasises the quality of general education provided by the schools, it also highlights the curricular and non-curricular contributions of that education to individual socialisation, to the development of attitudes and dispositions.

Efforts by radical critics to expose the way in which schools serve the needs and interests of capital [7] have, over the last five years, met countervailing attention from policy-makers and educators concerned to develop more positive attitudes towards capitalist economic arrangements. Such attitudes assume greater importance in the context of what has been called, in contrast to the 'invisible hand', the 'invisible handshake' – implicit agreements, not about the hours to be worked, but about the intensity and the quality of the labour offered. In the economists' language, labour contracts are incomplete [5]. Yet industrial relations legislation and the power of trade unions have weakened many of the traditional sanctions that influenced labour intensity. Economists acknowledge its importance as a factor in output per worker employed [22] but it is difficult to quantify.

Teaching is not an activity that can or should be subject to close supervision. As was discovered in countries that experienced foreign occupation, it is very difficult to control what teachers say and do when the classroom door is closed, let alone to specify the influence they exert on students' development and values. In the last analysis we have no choice but to trust our teachers.

Thus, suggestions that teachers are conveying a false picture of capitalism and of industrial conditions, past or present, evoke a strong response from the profession, and not just on behalf of the politically committed. The great majority of teachers are well aware that they have to eschew the blandishments of both left and right, particularly the view that since objectivity and balance are inherently impossible, it is better to make political standpoints explicit both to oneself and to students.

The conventions that govern political discourse and those relevant to teaching are different. Lectures and lessons on controversial subjects are not political speeches. The imperatives of free speech and free thought that Percy Nunn saw as needing protection in the 1930s still matter today. They are not well served by accounts of capitalism, of industrial development or, for that matter, of anything else, that are inadequately informed and which lack historical perspective. Yet there is no intrinsic reason why the encouragement of students' critical capacities, and clear-sightedness about the weaknesses as well as the strengths of different forms of social and economic organisation, in the hands of competent and well-informed teachers, should lead to rejection of the values of the society that permits and encourages such criticism. The danger of indoctrination from one direction is not best dealt with by substituting equal and opposite influences, but by ensuring that teacher education and training develops knowledge, discrimination and judgement adequate to the responsibilities of the role. It is not so much bias as ignorance that leads to the depiction of industrial history in terms of flint-faced capitalists replacing kindly squires, reeking slums supplanting idyllic villages and economic man invariably acting as a hard-nosed short-run maximiser. As Dore [10] has recently suggested in relation to Japan, it is by no means certain that the productive success of our competitors *has* depended upon crude utility maximisation, nor do the followers of Ruskin have a monopoly of concern for the development of business ethics [15].

The pronouncements of those who would use education for purposes of propaganda or the class struggle offer good copy, but a poor return on our time and attention. The problem is not that teachers and students know or believe the wrong things, or are generally speaking opposed to capitalist values or economic success, but that they do not know enough. If education itself was more productive in terms of quality of knowledge and understanding [26,27] there might be fewer problems about its contribution to economic performance.

Conclusions for policy
The evidence of HMI Reports and large-scale surveys of current

educational practice and teacher opinion does not suggest that schools today espouse political and social values sharply at variance with those required for economic success. But neither, with some exceptions, are schools particularly active in directly stimulating changes in those attitudes which might be seen as making for improved economic performance. Self-conscious efforts to influence long-standing social evaluations, such as the status of industrial versus professional employment, and to rescue profit, trade and commerce from judgements based on reaction to the excesses of nineteenth century industrialisation, can have only limited success unless corresponding changes are taking place outside the schools. To an increasing extent over the past decade, they have been. The Manpower Services Commission and its various schemes are now such a ubiquitous part of the national scene, and expenditure on their activities is now so large, that it is easy to forget that the Commission is only just ten years old. Links between MSC schemes and the educational system have recently been increased, particularly in further education and as a result of the Technical and Vocational Education Initiative (TVEI). Yet the Commission's work is still largely separate from that of the Department of Education and Science and the local authorities that maintain schools and employ teachers.

The reasons for such separation are familiar enough. Administratively, training has been linked with employment rather than with education. Politically, governments have been somewhat less than satisfied with the way in which secondary schools have dealt with their older age groups. Financially, it has been difficult to earmark for particular purposes the funds made available to local authorities. Managerially, effective training has been regarded as needing central direction and control. But more fundamentally, the separation reflects the way in which history, economic circumstances and social structure have given us a heritage of values, attitudes and assumptions that constitute education and training as two separate metaphors, a heritage which continues to influence our thought and our practice.

It is not difficult to identify the values conventionally associated with these two metaphors. Education is often depicted as soft, person-centred, moralised, academic, critical, contemplative, radical in attitude but traditional in form, theoretical, norm-referenced, enclosed, a consumption good rather than an investment. In contrast, training is represented as hard, task-centred, materialistic, practical, oriented towards action, criterion-referenced, pragmatic, innovative in structure but conservative in substance, unselective, open, a valuable national investment.

The distinctions that underpin the separate value systems of education and training may already have been weakened by ten years of the Manpower Services Commission; the impact of activities such as 'Understanding British Industry' (now involving nearly four thousand secondary schools and some seventy local authorities); the scheme for professional, industrial and commercial updating (PICKUP); the Curriculum Council's Industry Project; 'Education for Capability'; college-employer links projects (CELP); and the appointment of a large number of industrial liaison officers.

Several themes now command support across the whole political spectrum. Raising standards of literacy and numeracy is acknowledged as a condition for acquiring new knowledge and skills and greater flexibility in adjusting to technological and social change. (Literacy is seen as neutral in relation to social and political values. It was not always so.) The part that high quality, trained leadership in schools can play in creating favourable learning and teaching conditions is at last being widely recognised. There are new, and I trust welcome, developments in teacher education and training. But there are still areas – for example, independent education, selectivity, secondary school examinations, the respective roles of central and local government and the possibility of reform in our creaking (and divisive) system of transfer payments – where greater effort to generate and to profit from serious non-partisan debate is needed if a sufficiently broad basis of support for change is to be developed.

There has as yet been no great enthusiasm to face the implications of chronic unemployment for the induction of citizens into political and social values, a process hitherto dependent in part on the disciplines of the work-place, or the risks of calling into being an apathetic 'underclass'. The lessons of the kinds of political and economic behaviour commented upon by, for example, Beer [4], Dahrendorf [9] and Olson [19] – the fragmentation of British political life, its perception as a zero-sum game, the difficulty of maintaining sensible policies in the face of the self-defeating logic of short-run self-interest – are having to be learned in more painful ways than most educators would have chosen. Sadly, calls for greater understanding of and commitment to higher-order values do not carry conviction; they resonate too strongly of the 1930s, and of a society in which wages and profits were seen as mutually antagonistic rather than complementary.

High labour substitutability, the dangers of trained incapacity, unpredictable futures and a new balance of industrial and service employment all caution against the belief that stronger vocational and technological emphases in education and training will *in themselves* contribute significantly to improved productivity and economic performance. Levels of labour intensity and a concern for the quality of products and of services offered are influenced by attitudes and values, by socialisation as much as by training in skills. Attempts to teach attitudes and values, unless mediated through attested public traditions of worthwhile knowledge, under the guidance of well educated and competent teachers, are readily politicised and vulnerable to charges of indoctrination. Can we identify and modify the values that underpin and legitimate unproductive practices and strengthen those likely to contribute to improved productivity, without sacrificing what is of enduring value within our existing social, cultural and educational traditions? It is this challenge that any useful discussion of education and economic performance must confront.

References

[1] Aldcroft, D.H., 'Britain's economic decline 1870–1980' in Roderick, G.W. and Stephens, M. (ed), *The British Malaise*, Brighton, The Falmer Press, 1982.

[2] Anthony, P.D., *John Ruskin's Labour: a Study of Ruskin's Social Theory*, Cambridge University Press, 1983.

[3] Barker, R., *Education and Politics 1900–1951: a Study of the Labour Party*, Oxford, Clarendon Press, 1972.

[4] Beer, S.H., *Britain against Itself: the Political Contradictions of Collectivism*, London, Faber, 1982.

[5] Blaug, M., 'Where are we now in the economics of education', Paris, OECD, mimeo, 1972.

[6] Board of Education *Regulations for Secondary Schools* 1904, in Maclure, J.S., *Educational Documents, England and Wales 1816 to the present*, London, Methuen, 1978.

[7] Bowles, S. and Gintis, H., *Schooling in Capitalist America*, London, Routledge and Kegan Paul, 1976.

[8] Cowling, M., *Religion and Public Doctrine in Modern England*, Cambridge University Press, 1981.

[9] Dahrendorf, R., *On Britain*, London, British Broadcasting Corporation, 1982.

[10] Dore, R., 'Goodwill and the spirit of market capitalism', *British Journal of Sociology*, 1982.

[11] Greenough, A.H. and Crofts, F., *Theory and Practice in the new Secondary Schools*, London, University of London Press, 1945.

[12] Gosden, P., *The Education System since 1944*, Oxford, Martin Robertson, 1983.

[13] Heyck, T.W., *The Transformation of Intellectual Life in Victorian England*, London, Croom Helm, 1982.

[28] Wiener, M., *English Culture and the Decline of the Industrial Spirit*, Cambridge University Press, 1981.

[15] Matthews, R.C.O., 'Morality, competition and efficiency', *The Manchester School*, XLIX:4, 1981.

[16] Matthews, R.C.O., Feinstein, C.H. and Odling-Smee, J.C., *British Economic Growth, 1985–1973*, Oxford, Clarendon Press, 1982.

[17] Norman, E., 'Establishment thinking as a threat to capitalism', *Times Higher Education Supplement*, 13 May, 1977.

[18] Nunn, P., 'Remaking the secondary school', in Rawson, E. (ed), *The Freedom We Seek*, London, New Education Fellowship, 1937.

[19] Olson, M., *The Rise and Decline of Nations: Economic Growth, Stagflation and Social Rigidities*, New Haven, Yale University Press, 1982.

[20] Percy, E., *Some Memories*, London, 1958 (quoted Jeffries, K., Lord Eustace Percy, the Conservative Party and the Education of the Adolescent (unpublished manuscript), 1984.

[21] Pollard, S., *The Wasting of the British Economy: British Economic Policy, 1945 to the present*, London, Croom Helm, 1982.

[22] Pearson, R., *Qualified Manpower in Employment*, Brighton, Institute of Manpower Studies, 1976.

[23] Pearson, R., 'The new technologies: the responsiveness of higher education to manpower needs', Paper for the 1983 Conference of the Society for Research in Higher Education, Guildford, The Society, 1983.

[24] Roderick, G.W. and Stephens, M. (eds), *Where did we go wrong? Industrial Performance, Education and the Economy in Victorian Britain*, Brighton, Falmer Press, 1981.

[25] Roderick, G.W. and Stephens, M. (eds), *The British Malaise*, Brighton, Falmer Press, 1982.

[26] Walberg, H.J., Harnisch, D., Tsa, S–L, 'High school productivity in twelve countries', *Journal of Educational Research*, 1984.

[27] Waxman, H.C. and Walberg, H.J., 'The relation of teaching and learning: a review of reviews', *Contemporary Education Review*, 1982:2.

[28] Wiener, M., *English Culture and the Decline of the Industrial Spirit*, Cambridge University Press, 1981.

10 The Responsiveness of the Education System to Change
by Stuart Maclure

Introduction

This chapter is about the capacity of the education system to respond to changing public demand, the way in which such a response is made and the nature of the influences which speed it up or slow it down. These matters are never far below the surface in discussions on education policy, especially when there is a surge of popular criticism.

It is by no means clear to me that our schools are preturnaturally unresponsive to change, as previously alleged. Examples can be given of ways in which schools and the educational system have responded quickly – some would say too quickly – to external stimuli: it is another commonplace to charge the schools with an excessive susceptibility to fashionable educational ideas and nostrums.

The formulation of the discussion is such as to encourage centralist presumptions. 'What ought we to do about so and so?' always envisages a 'we' of centralising tendency and authoritarian disposition. I want to make it clear at the outset that I am not a centralist and do not believe the Department of Education and Science could get better answers out of the school system than the local education authorities. Nor do I believe that a system of decentralised central government on the lines of the National Health Service would be a good way to run the schools.

Schooling and society

The point of departure has to be the network of links which connect what happens in education to what is happening in society. Education is a subordinate activity which depends on larger social and cultural priorities. Insofar as it is largely paid for from public funds and managed by public bodies, it is subject in outline to public control. But education is also an activity in which there is direct public participation. Every family with children participates if only by being part of the community of a particular school. The content and practice of education is influenced, therefore, at every level by the culture and mores of the society in which it is embedded. The degree to which this culture and these mores are articulated by the central government or by local authorities differs from country to country and from age to age; in Britain it differs as between England and Wales, and Scotland. The present happens to be a time when the Government is being drawn into the business of giving greater definition to the curriculum, at the national level, than had become customary. This is no more than the reassertion and extension of a national role, set aside by the Government before and after the Second World War.

What happens in school, therefore, is the result of a mixture of competing pressures: (a) those exerted or not exerted by the Government in the form of a state curriculum; (b) those projected by the teaching profession; (c) those applied by the examination system which reflect both the priorities determined by the Government and those of higher education; (d) those brought into the schools by the pupils, directly, and by their parents, indirectly; (e) those formed by the expectations which the local community loads on to the school. To these should be added the social and cultural influences of the media, insofar as they cause to resonate the dominant themes of the time, not only in terms of high culture, but also in popular music, TV and newspapers.

Labour market pressures exert an influence through (a), (d) and (e) as well as through the Careers Service and careers teaching in the secondary schools. For those whom the schools see as most successful, careers choice, as opposed to just getting a job, is linked to higher or further education and is largely conditional upon fairly conventional academic progress, as monitored and steered by the examination system. For the majority, whose career options (at 16, at any rate) will be limited to openings which do not depend on specified examination pre-qualifications, the relevant labour markets are much more local, and the flow of information about employment – and unemployment – will come to the school, formally, via the Careers Service and informally via the experience of previous generations of school leavers and from parents and siblings.

The adaptability of the system as a whole
On the broader canvas, it is arguable that education has reflected, only too closely, the larger developments of society. This seems to me to be the burden of the Correlli Barnett thesis and the Martin Wiener argument: far from showing that educational institutions were at odds with the society which was developing in the nineteenth century, Barnett and Wiener show how faithfully the schools mirrored the values which dominated British society.

What has happened has clearly represented a triumph for latent, dominant, cultural values over the more superficial attempts by politicians and admininstrators to steer educational development in a different direction. It is the strenuous efforts made by politicians and educational administrators in the last 30 years of the nineteenth century which give piquancy to the arguments put forward by Barnett and Wiener. Some of those who occupied positions of power in the system, from Prince Albert onwards, saw clearly the shortcomings of English industry and the role of the English educational system in perpetuating these. The right lessons were freely drawn from the German education system and money was channelled into technical education. But the institutions which were created as a result of these initiatives failed to achieve high status, or else achieved it only by changing into something else.

In her Wilkins Lecture, Professor Margaret Gowing [4] discussed five suggested causes for the failure of the efforts of these Victorian educational reformers: money (or rather, the lack of it); administrative structure; social class; the influence of the Church; and imperial purpose (which she is inclined to set aside).

Within this list, social class is a surrogate for the larger preoccupations of the dominant groups in society which caused successful manufacturers to set their hearts on the gentrification of their sons and daughters. The causes were not to be explained narrowly in terms of the responsiveness of individual institutions or units of Government, central or local, but in the climate of opinion within which institutions and officials had to live and move and have their being. The politicians were not strong enough or single-minded enough to confront and change the pattern of ideas which formed this dominant climate.

The parallels with the late twentieth century are obvious as Martin Wiener forcefully pointed out [1]. If the social assumptions built into the education system are rooted deep down in a pattern of values which reflect these same anti-entrepreneurial priorities it would require a 'cultural revolution', 'a very un-English ideological fierceness', to bring about a shift.

The time-scale for any major change of direction in the education system adds to the difficulty of engineering change and the likelihood that the schools and colleges will be presented with conflicting messages which will paralyse their responses. The present secondary education system is in the mess it is in for the lack of coherent direction. The change from a system of separate grammar, technical and secondary modern schools to comprehensive schools has taken place over a period of more than forty years and is still not complete. During that period the political pendulum has produced alternating periods of activity and paralysis, legislation and the repeal of legislation, which have faithfully reflected the continuing divisions in public opinion. Even more important has been the maintenance within the education sytem of a number of contradictions, derived from the resolute defence of a highly selective and academically elitist university system, alongside a nascent system of comprehensive secondary education.

Where the Swedes, when they planned their comprehensive secondary system, considered study content and the organisational structure of schools together, the English pretended that the sole issue lay in the method of allocating pupils to schools; the key phrase was negative – 'abolishing the 11-plus'. In curriculum terms, the implication was that the comprehensive school would simply combine under one roof all the courses (and examination syllabuses) which had hitherto been provided separately. There was no available consensual foundation on which to erect any other comprehensive school structure. The weakness of the reasoning has become increasingly obvious as time has passed.

The present contradictions of the secondary curriculum seem to require either a full-blooded acceptance of the logic of comprehensive education and the major development of post-secondary education and vocational training which should follow it (as it has done in North America and Scandinavia), or a reversion to more highly differentiated secondary curricula geared, as now, to elitist higher education and a stratified system of post-secondary technical and vocational education. Neither of these radical options is seriously on offer; instead, there is merely a modest attempt to tidy up the present disarray.

Teaching and curriculum

It is against this background that the responsiveness of the system to more specific demands for change needs to be assessed. If, for example, there were some clearly identifiable change in practice which would lead to better learning by pupils throughout the system or in some specific part of it, and this could be clearly and cogently articulated, how could this be introduced? Is the system capable of giving a systematic response?

Any attempt to probe these questions is bound to be discursive and inconclusive. Educational research has produced few immediately marketable ideas or strategies. There is, for example, no 'best' way to teach children to read. Teachers, it seems, are most effective when they have arrived at their own compromises, based on their own experiences. Initial and in-service training may help them to do this intelligently, but there is no simple formula which could be imposed with confidence from the centre, even supposing the necessary administrative authority existed.

It could be argued, perhaps, that any single method, universally applied, might be more efficient because it would make it easier for pupils to transfer from school to school and class to class. But it is also extremely likely that bureaucratic uniformity would limit the ability of the teacher to adapt to circumstances which are far from uniform with regard to the linguistic development of pupils, the demands made on the teachers and their own differing levels of skill.

The rapidly mounting pile of published HMI reports on primary and secondary schools dilate on a series of themes relating to the good management of schools and the practice of good teaching. HMIs dwell on teachers' expectations of pupil performance; on the range of work and activities needed to extend pupils of all abilities to the full; on the need for business-like teaching schemes; on the balance held by the teachers between examinable and non-examinable work; on the quality of the relationships between staff and pupils, and between senior and junior staff.

It is a favourite platitude to observe that educational standards could be hoisted if more of the less successful schools could be brought up to the level of the average. This is one of those statements of the obvious which nevertheless conceals some elementary truths. The feasibility of such an aim is supported by evidence of the kind mustered by Michael Rutter and his colleagues in their study of some London comprehensives [6]. This suggested that some of the differences between schools which had 'good' results and those which had 'bad' results could be linked to some simple measures of managerial efficiency like punctuality and absenteeism on the part of teachers and pupils, the setting and marking of homework, the noise level in class, the distribution of praise and blame and so on. Many of the findings followed common sense: pupils did better in more orderly surround- ings, where work was taken seriously and time was not wasted.

This widely expressed concern about school management and the standard of teaching points to action of two kinds. The first is in-service training; the second is personnel managment.

In-service training
Nothing suggests that there are any short cuts to improvement. Something can be done to give heads more training in managerial skills: hence the interest in staff development aimed at improving the capacity of heads, especially of large secondary schools, to manage their staff and direct their efforts towards clearly stated objectives. Indeed, there is a history of not very determined, not very successful, in-service training for heads, the latest and most serious developments coming in the form of a programme announced by the Secretary of State in December 1982, drawing on funding powers provided under a long overlooked clause of the 1962 Education Act. Local education authorities and heads are likely to cooperate to the full – in that sense, the system will certainly respond: how far the training will be effective in changing the way people think and act will be a matter for careful evaluation later on.

Post-experience training for all teachers has also figured repeatedly in the prescriptions for raising educational standards, most notably, perhaps, in the James Report [2] of 1972, which regarded a large and continuing programme of in-service education for teachers as, in many ways, more important than anything which could be done to improve initial training. In practice, however, the provision and uptake of in-service training has consistently fallen short of the Government's hopes. The absence (until the 1962 Act came to be invoked for certain kinds of course) of any directly earmarked funds for this purpose has meant that in-service training has been only one item among all the others in a local education authority budget: in the competition for funds, authorities (under pressure from teachers' unions) have generally preferred to spend money to keep teachers in front of classes, rather than to release them for additional training. It has to be said, too, that the quality of the in-service training on offer has been of variable quality.

The messages the local authorities receive about keeping down costs as a whole are much stronger than those which urge more in-service training. What emerges at the end reflects the combination of all these promptings, tempered by the personal qualities and enthusiasms of senior local politicians and educational administrators.

As for the teachers, the messages which they hear reflect, in part, their interests as an occupational group whose prime concern is to protect teaching jobs; but only in part: they also have the interest of their pupils at heart and are unpersuaded of the value of much of the in-service training on offer. And they, too, have lines out to parents and governors and probably have a better idea of their priorities than Westminster politicians or senior civil servants.

The planned increase in central government spending on teachers' courses may well be matched by even less willingness on the part of local authorities to incur local expenditure on similar activities; if the Government seems inclined to take over responsibility for this, the authorities may well feel disposed, in the present economic climate, to let it get on with it. Many kinds of in-service training need to be done on a local basis with the close involvement of local authority advisory staff. This, in itself, means that there are manpower implications which neither the Government nor the local authorities are able to face up to and which will become even more pressing if local advisers are to be increasingly occupied with the relocation of secondary staff in the face of falling pupil rolls.

Personnel management

Given the fact that there are 104 local education authorities in England and Wales, 30,000 schools and 450,000 teachers, there must always be scope for improvement in the deployment and management of the professional staff. It is clear that there is much more to the difficulties of schools in many areas than can be remedied by telling teachers to pull their socks up. However, tougher management is undoubtedly one element in the Governments's proposed strategy, as set out in the White Paper on *Teaching Quality* [3]. A good case can be made out for better procedures, including regular assessment of teachers for the purpose of staff development and selection for promotion and, if current negotiations come to fruition, merit awards for classroom teachers. The Secretary of State has, on a number of occasions, made pointed references to the need to weed out ineffective teachers. This is also referred to in the White Paper.

For fairly obvious reasons there has been little sign that 'the system' is responding kindly to these suggestions of a tougher management style. Teachers are no more eager than civil servants or professional staff in the National Health Service to surrender their normal employment safeguards. Proving 'incompetence' against a teacher is seldom easy except in egregious cases. The teacher's tenure is not absolute in the sense that some university teachers have their rights enshrined in ancient (or modern) charters, but they usually have detailed disciplinary procedures laid down, involving hearings before various local tribunals or local authority sub-committees. Because it is a serious matter to take away someone's professional livelihood, there is a heavy burden of proof on the administrators who seek to remove a teacher from his post. Even in a large local educational authority with a strong administration, it is simply not practical on grounds of staff time alone, as things now stand, to envisage more than a handful of cases in any year.

Falling rolls and premature retirement have made it easier, particularly in the case of heads and department heads, to encourage unsuccessful teachers to bow out gracefully. But, although it is suggested from time to time that steps should be taken to make 'less effective' teachers redundant as the total demand for teachers falls, it is by no means clear that this could be done formally as a matter of policy, rather than informally through the operation of the present early retirement arrangements. Codes of practice on redundancy make 'last in, first out' a defensible position for an employer to adopt: redundancy which takes the form of a unilateral picking and choosing by the employer is altogether more dubious and potentially unfair.

What is clearly needed is a properly funded, voluntary, redundancy scheme based on length of service which could offer release to ineffective teachers trapped in the wrong job, much sooner than any early retirement scheme now available. It would, of course, have to make the right to take redundancy subject to the operating requirements of the system.

It is an illusion to believe that ordinary competent teachers wish to protect the handful of incompetents who make trouble for their colleagues as well as short-change the pupils. This does not mean, however, that they would stand for authoritarian edicts from the Secretary of State or anyone else, tinged as the rhetoric of Ministers has so often been, on this subject, with that profound contempt for school teachers which Ministers, mandarins and industrial managers all have in common. For some reason there is a psychological trap which opens before those with the high intellectual gifts needed to reach senior ranks in the civil service. Aware that their own gifts would be unlikely to keep them afloat in the fourth form of an inner city comprehensive school for more than five minutes, they nevertheless find it easy to pontificate on the competence of those who, week in, week out, have to try to kindle a spark of interest and commitment in a streetwise generation weaned of the deference which once provided schoolmasters and mistresses with an external authority.

The two largest unions of schoolteachers belong to the TUC: the National Union of Teachers affiliated in May 1970 and the National Association of Schoolmasters/Union of Women Teachers in November 1968. The NUT, in particular, take TUC membership seriously, value their seat on the General Council and seek to line up TUC backing for their educational views. Yet in terms of industrial action, the teachers' unions are weak: the strike is, for them, a weapon of strictly limited value because their middle class members have mortgages and other commitments which mean that their unions can only call them out if they pay their full salaries. The teachers' unions are democratically run with strict rules about balloting before action and, in the case of the National Union of Teachers, in particular, firm measures are taken against members or groups which engage in unofficial action.

The ambiguous nature of the teachers' professional status is reflected in their salaries. About a quarter of all teachers receive less than the national average manual and non-manual gross weekly earnings and those teachers within the hierarchy of senior posts who are among the best paid 10 per cent – heads, deputies and other senior staff – only receive about one and a half times the national average.

These salary levels are low by comparison with teachers in European countries, such as Sweden and Germany, though simple comparisons can be misleading. The size of the teaching force makes it extremely unlikely that the level of remuneration will be dramatically raised; on two occasions salaries have been jacked up – by the Houghton and Clegg awards in 1974 and 1980 – and in the years which followed the gains were guickly lost and former relativities were reasserted.

Curriculum

If teaching and teaching quality is one leg on which proposals for improvement stand, the second leg is curriculum change.

The present Secretary of State, continuing the strategy worked out in the DES between 1976 and 1980, is seeking to give greater definition to the curriculum by causing the examination boards to set out their requirements for the various grades at GCE and CSE in terms of specific tasks and operations, with the intention of using these criteria as a basis for tightly drawn school syllabuses. He is thus counting on

Table 10.1   *Schoolteachers' earnings:* [a] *Great Britain, 1983*

£ per week

	Primary teachers	Secondary teachers	All manual and non-manual employees
Full-time men (per cent)			
Lowest 10	131.90	131.70	96.30
Lower 25	160.00	154.40	118.40
Median	180.70	190.50	150.30
Upper 25	211.70	217.80	195.00
Top 10	237.70	241.60	255.00
Average gross weekly earnings	184.60	188.50	167.50
Sample number	452	1409	
Full-time women			
Lowest 10	121.60	120.30	65.60
Lower 25	140.30	135.60	78.70
Median	162.10	160.40	98.80
Upper 25	177.80	187.40	128.30
Top 10	200.90	217.30	166.20
Average gross weekly earnings	160.90	163.10	108.80
Sample number	1431	1179	

Sample number x average earnings for each of the above yields:

Average weekly earnings of teachers in regular service	£172.57
Average weekly earnings of males over 21 and females over 18 in all industries	£148.30

Source: New Earnings Survey, 1983, Part D, Analysis by occupation, Tables 96 and 97, 99 and 100, and Employment *Gazette* December 1983, Table 5.6, page 550 for the £148.30 figure.

[a] New Earnings Survey data relate to gross pay, before tax and national insurance contributions have been deducted. Figures above cover those whose pay period was not affected by absence. The 4.98 per cent Burnham settlement for 1983 was not included in the survey period. Other groups whose national settlements are not reflected in the figures include printing and mechanical construction workers, non-industrial civil servants and some workers of London Transport, British Steel Corporation and the Post Office.

most of the exercise in curriculum revision being undertaken by some sort of consensus among the groups of subject specialists and experts in assessment who now run the examination system. This expectation is probably justified: the exercise will enjoy a wide measure of support.

The DES has chosen the road to curriculum reform which fits in most easily with the decentralised administrative system. The snags are not hard to see. The negative educational consequences of allowing examinations to dominate the curriculum are regularly reported by HMIs. The latest changes proposed by the DES will make examinations still more important and positively encourage teachers to subordinate all their activities to the overriding need to satisfy the ever more specific demands of the examiners.

Other education systems, with less decentralised forms of administration, survive with little or no external examining at the end of the compulsory school period (but with formal systems of internal examining) because they have centrally determined curricula laid down in documents which may well require Parliamentary approval.

In theory, a strong centralised system like the French, or a system based on strong units of regional or provincial government like the German *länder* which act, centrally, within their regions, has more control over the curriculum, more power to institute change in the content and method of study. Certainly, where centralised curriculum control is linked to financial control, it is – again theoretically – much easier to initiate 'total' change in the sense of rewriting the curriculum, retraining the teachers, revising the text books, re-equipping the schools, remodelling the examinations and modifying entry regulations to higher education, apprenticeship or whatever.

In practice, of course, there are obstacles as well as easements. A great deal depends on the size of the system. The facility for system-wide change is much greater in a country like Sweden where the total population is comparable with that of Greater London, than in France, where Napoleonic centralism does not seem to have made it particularly easy to carry through the succession of changes which have been projected in recent years.

'Total' change, is, by definition, expensive and if all the responsibility and the financial obligation is vested in the Government, the cost implications of new policies are easily calculated and set aside. Centralised systems, like decentralised, are liable to have to make do with pilot projects and hope, often against hope, that the lessons learnt under ideal conditions in a well funded pilot project will somehow be absorbed without cost by the less well endowed rest of the system.

However, as Bob Moon [5] has shown in a comparison of curriculum reform in mathematics in the 1960s and 1970s in five countries (Britain, Germany, France, Denmark and the Netherlands), centralised systems do not necessarily behave as the rule book would suggest they should. The processes of dissemination of 'new' mathematics in the 1960s were remarkably similar in centralised France and decentralised Britain. Strong central decision-making did not ensure the acceptance of controversial policies. Much of the running was made by teachers and book publishers. The authorities found themselves running to catch up with practice which was moving down into the schools from higher education. Moon found a similar pattern in Denmark and the German *länd* of Hessen and concluded that curriculum changes in the 1980s may, similarly, turn on influences which 'transcend any national contexts' and reflect wider political, economic and social developments.

In spite of the attempts of the curriculum theorists and the technocrats of instruction to establish a conceptual framework which could accommodate the experience of teachers in different education systems and different social traditions, unsurprisingly, it has become clear that while, technically, many of the curriculum issues in Western Europe, North America and Japan, are similar, there are no answers which necessarily apply to all, though, one by one, they tend to move in the same direction.

Comparisons of standards in particular subjects (as, for example, in the National Institute studies) produce interesting results and raise sharp and uncomfortable questions. It is disturbing to find the gap in standards between what the Germans can demand of average and below average pupils in mathematics and the standards achieved by similar pupils in English schools. Similarly, there are strong indications that the Russians also set much higher targets for their average pupils than can realistically be envisaged here. As for the Japanese, they seem to outperform most others in international comparisons. It is, however, harder to offer explanations which separate with clarity the pedagogic and curricular factors from those which relate to the larger social context. There is no need to labour the point: if external social pressures of one kind or another are powerful enough, children will perform well, irrespective of curriculum or teaching method. As external social pressures are likely to determine the status of the teachers, the market value of examination certificates, the relationships between pupils and teachers, as well as the reinforcing power of parents, it is obvious that information about differences in academic performance and the content of study is unlikely to yield to simple interpretation.

Much of the published evidence about curriculum innovation in the 1960s and 1970s is less than encouraging. Simply telling teachers to do things differently does not seem to have been particularly effective. The most effective methods seem to have involved developing new teaching methods and teaching materials in participating pilot schools, backed with sufficient funding to cover the extra costs of books and equipment and outside consultants where necessary. But even the best R and D models have had limited success and the forces of inertia, reinforced by the accumulated training and experience invested in former methods which are now to be discarded, are very powerful.

The Government's new, examination-led, curriculum reform will not be the only consideration in the minds of those who run the schools. The teachers must also listen to the local education authorities, their employers and the statutory custodians of the curriculum. While successive governments have been amplifying their own attempts to evoke responses from teachers, they have also been urging local education authorities to review their own curricular policies. In such reviews the teachers have been intimately involved; in the process hearing – and contributing – nuances which may be different from those emanating from the DES.

Local authorities, being political institutions, include many which do not see eye-to-eye with the Government of the day and have their own priorities: for example some Labour-controlled authorities have demanded peace studies on the school timetable. Others, of various political persuasions, have bent the teachers' ears on multi-ethnic education, on the educational demands of an 'equal opportunities' policy, on school discipline without corporal punishment.

Practical approach

Alongside the proposals for better definition of the content of the secondary curriculum go other plans which reflect the Government's desire to emphasise vocational applications of theoretical knowledge, and to cultivate such concepts as 'capability' and the ability to apply knowledge to the solution of practical problems – the assumption being that the examination reform and curriculum development can, at the same time, accommodate a change of method and approach.

The main engine of reform in this respect is not the examination at 16-plus, but the pilot programme set up, financed and supervised by the Manpower Services Commission with the imposing title of the Technical and Vocational Education Initiative. Within two years 60 local education authorities have been signed up. The aim has been to give a sudden and forceful shock to the system by allowing a rich outside body to charge in where the DES has, until now, had no statutory authority.

Local authority responses have been mixed. Some, mainly Labour-controlled, disliked the method by which the scheme was bounced on the educational world, distrusted its MSC parentage and suspected its comprehensive bona fides. A majority of authorities, on the other hand, have gratefully seized the money and used it to support, extend and propagate programmes which were already in existence in a small way before TVEI was launched.

The education system's short-term response may, therefore, be characterised once again as patchy but not surprisingly so given the extreme haste in which the scheme was launched and the aggressive absence of consultation.

As to the longer-term response, this is much less easy to forecast because there is absolutely no indication of what will happen five years hence when TVEI ends and local authorities have to pick up the bills. All the snags of the pilot project approach can be seen on the horizon; the contrast between the enthusiasm raised by a new experimental programme, backed up by large sums of additional money for extra staff and expensive equipment and the return to reality when the special funding ends and normal service is resumed.

There is no reason to suppose that the teachers are obstructive to the new initiative, nor yet that the opposition of the dissident local education authorities is implacable.

The response of 'the system' to the various initiatives aimed at changing the curricular priorities of primary and secondary schools will depend in large measure on the consistency with which these priorities are stated over a period of time.

Many people would regard the need to replace narrow academic attitudes with a broader, more practical approach as one of the most important and ambitious of the current aims set out by the Secretary of State for Education. But already it is possible to detect differences between rhetoric and reality. The rhetoric is that this new, relevant, practical approach should be for all; the bright as well as the dull, the O- and A-level groups as well as the CSEs. And so, one suspects, Ministers genuinely believe. But sixth form teachers and sixth formers will know that entry to universities has become more competitive and that, in spite of all the evidence about the poor predictive quality of A-levels, university departments are forced to base their admission policies on rigid interpretation of A-level results. With only a handful of marks dividing a B grade from a D grade, what sixth form teacher or intelligent sixth former is going to be governed by Ministerial rhetoric if this means letting up on the single-minded pursuit of the entry qualification? And the same pressures extend lower and lower down the schools as O-levels come into play in the distribution of conditional university places for pupils in the fourth term of the sixth form. Already the change in Oxford entry methods are causing independent schools which once could afford to be fairly relaxed about O-levels, to re-think their strategy.

Conclusions

Policy-making

It is conventional to describe the English education system as a partnership and to identify the partners as the DES, the local education authorities and the teachers, to whom it might now be appropriate to add the parents. This has a whiff of consensus politics about it. It expresses the thinking behind the 1944 Education Act and the practice of the first twenty years of its operation when the Act itself provided an acceptable outline of consensual policy. In the present political climate consensus is no longer a fashionable idea, but still the distribution of power and influence within the educational system, sooner or later, obliges Secretaries of State, no matter how abrasive they would like to be, to try to build as wide a coalition of support as possible. Without it they cannot hope to achieve their objectives.

The need for a measure of consensus is a reflection of the decentralisation of the system and the time-scale of educational reform, which (as with the policies promulgated by Sir Keith Joseph at the North of England Conference) extends far beyond the four or five year span between general elections.

One priority in any attempt to improve the responsiveness of the education system would be a serious study of educational policy-making and how to broaden its base. This might suggest the need for more serious policy study outside the DES which would also help in the process of re-charging the batteries of opposition parties who, otherwise, tend to entrust their own policy rethinking to such sectarian groups as happen to have the ear of the leadership. It would be important to feed into such studies relevant information about practice in other developed countries.

Finance

The present mechanisms of local government finance impose severe limitations on national education policy because there is no way, except by invoking outside agencies like the MSC, that policy-makers in central government can guarantee that funds will be allocated to carry out their aims.

This is a simple consequence of the block grant procedures of local government finance. It is exacerbated by the breakdown of any accepted view about public expenditure and the punitive measures which central government has felt obliged to take in the attempt to maintain overall control of local government spending. In 'normal' times it has been possible for central and local government to live with a shared understanding of the main aims of policy and the priorities which go with them. But such 'normal' times may have gone for good.

The new Education Support Grants which will permit the DES to have direct control over a sum equivalent to ½ per cent of the expenditure covered by the rate support grant will, for the first time, give Elizabeth House a small development fund; a sure way of getting direct responses from local education authorities, who will pocket their pride along with the DES handout. There must be a temptation for the DES to seek to increase the proportion of total funding distributed through education support grants to pay for the continuation and extension of TVEI, but only in the face of more fierce battles with the local authorities.

There is an obvious need for close attention to be paid to the future mechanisms of local government and local government finance with special regard to the various services provided by local authorities. Education may be the service most directly affected by the dichotomy between policy and finance. Ad hoc attempts to patch up the present arrangements clearly cannot last indefinitely.

Teachers and teachers' unions

Serious consideration needs to be given to ways of raising the morale and status of teachers. Having reached a similar conclusion, a number of American states have been discussing plans to raise teachers' salaries. California and Florida have approved such schemes. Merit payments to selected teachers figure in some of these revised pay schemes, generally opposed by teachers' unions which regard them as open to abuse and likely to provide an excuse for leaving the salaries of the mass of the profession depressed. Others involve the introduction of 'master teacher' grades for teachers who combine classroom teaching with wider curriculum and other responsibilities, some of which have hitherto implied (in the United States context) a transfer from the teaching staff to the administration.

Some years ago there was talk in this country of elevating the status of an elite group of class teachers by creating an underclass of teaching ancillaries. Without any serious proposals being discussed such notions faded away amid teachers' union protests about dilution and second class citizens. There remains a widely recognised need (acknowledged in the White Paper on *Teaching Quality* [3]) to adjust the teachers' salary scheme to enable more teachers of outstanding ability to be paid more without requiring them to move out of the classroom and spend more of their time on administration. It is likely that before agreeing to such a scheme, the employers will want a new definition of the teachers' contractual duties and some resolution of the long-running dispute over responsibility for the supervision of pupils at midday.

Better initial and in-service training is certainly needed. The present emphasis on the teacher's role as an instructor may be useful provided it is not carried too far. There ought to be a conscious effort to apply the results of research into the effectiveness of different teaching methods more directly to the training of teachers. It may well be that more research could be focused on specific instructional problems.

The influence of teachers' unions is considerable at the formal level when local authorities are seeking to introduce changes. Then union representatives can be helpful or they can hinder. They are always likely to be most active in matters which affect teachers' terms and conditions of service. This means that they are bound to come into play on questions of teacher redeployment for falling rolls. On such matters (as in London) they can be highly obstructive, especially if they are committed to a defence of a given number of teaching posts irrespective of the projected number of pupils.

It is also true that teachers' unions are useful scapegoats in the discussions of education policy: their influence and importance should not be exaggerated.

Parents

Parents represent the joker in the pack, the potential counterweight to the professionals, the potential ally of the politicians in the populist campaign for more relevant schools and higher standards.

Parents have been brought on to governing bodies under statute. They have had their right to express a preference in the choice of their children's schools spelt out with greater clarity. Ministers clearly hope they will help to underwrite the changes in the curriculum which are now under way.

It is important to distinguish between flattering parents for electoral reasons and mobilising them in the interest of effective schools. Up to now, all the attempts to enhance the influence of parents on governing bodies have also enhanced the influence of teachers.

Here, too, there is room for more study and experiment. More active parents must make for a more lively school community. It is not obvious, however, that the messages which the parents send out will coincide with those which come from the Government and the local education authorities. Some healthy controversy would be no bad thing, but from the point of view of a centralist seeking ways of bringing those on the periphery to heel, giving more power to parents does not sound like the ultimate answer.

References
[1] Alison, L, 'Is Britain's decline a myth?', *New Society*, 17 November 1983, pp. 274–5.
[2] Department of Education and Science, *Teacher Education and Training*, a report by a Committee of Inquiry appointed by the Secretary of State for

Education and Science, under the Chairmanship of Lord James of Rusholme, London, HMSO, 1973.

[3] Department of Education and Science, White Paper on *Teaching Quality*, *Cmnd* 8836, London, HMSO, 1983.

[4] Gowing, M., 'Science, technology and education: England in 1870', The Wilkins Lecture 1976, *Notes and Records of the Royal Society*, No. 32, pp. 71–90.

[5] Moon, Bob, 'Myths and reality in curriculum control', Galton, M. and Moon, Bob, (eds), *Changing Schools...Changing Curriculum*, London, Harper and Row, 1983.

[6] Rutter, M., Maughan, B., Mortimore, P., Ouston, J. and Smith, A., *Fifteen Thousand Hours: Secondary Schools and their effects on Children*, London, Open Books, 1979.

Comments on Chapters 8–10
by Mark Blaug

I must say that it is not easy to know what to make of the results reported by Postlethwaite. Let me begin by paying tribute to the work of IEA. IEA has long been a pioneer of international comparative education research. It was among the first to base its findings on nationally representative probability samples and to analyse the data by multivariate statistical analysis. It was also among the first to mobilise local research institutions in designing and collecting the data thus creating an unique worldwide decentralised institutional structure to coordinate comparative educational research. Finally, while much of its work, like the research reported here, concentrates on cognitive learning in schools, it has recently launched into a study of the effective behavioural outcomes of schools.

The work of the IEA has sometimes been criticised for its use of the so-called 'variance-partitioning method' of estimating the effects of inputs into the educational process, which fails to provide policy makers with any practical guidance on how to alter outcomes by manipulating inputs. A preferable statistical technique is ordinary or two-stage least squares, more common with economists than with psychometricians, but even here the IEA has recently shown itself willing to explore alternative statistical methods for analysing its data.

Be that as it may, what is revealed by the Postlethwaite evidence before us? We are presented with five bits of evidence on cognitive achievements for 13 and 14 year olds in (1) science and reading comprehension in the year 1970 and (2) mathematics in the year 1981. Whether we look at the mean score, the median score, or the variance of scores for the entire sample or for the lower half of the total sample, the results are invariably the same: England compares poorly with

Scotland, Sweden, Germany, the United States, Hungary and Japan; on all the comparisons, it is either the worst or almost the worst performer.

The problem with drawing inferences from these findings are (1) that the first set of figures pertaining to 1970 capture the effect of a secondary school system that was roughly half way between the old tripartite selective system and the new more or less totally comprehensivised system, whereas the 1981 figures reflect the consequences of almost universal comprehensivisation of English secondary education – in short, the two data sets are not comparable; and (2) that all the figures pertain to 13 and 14 year olds, that is, the age at which the English educational system begins to separate children into those expected to leave at 16 and those destined for post-compulsory schooling, the former being provided with a fairly general curriculum and the latter with an extremely specialised one – in short, it could be argued that the system is better judged at age 16 and not at age 13 or 14. Nevertheless, there is little comfort in the evidence even when we allow for all the ifs and buts.

Yes, but what follows, particularly for the problem before us, the education of 16–19 year olds? I confess that I don't know except that I am prepared to agree that English primary and lower secondary schools are worse than I thought. Postlethwaite invites us to speculate and proposes a national curriculum development centre, a national examination body, and compulsory in-service training for teachers. But I would want to precede those suggestions by a thorough overhaul of the O and A-level examination system. After all, the English educational system is unique in the world in the extent to which it compels a quarter to a third of the secondary school population to specialise in half a dozen subjects at the age of 14 and two or three subjects at the age of 16. No other country in the world specialises so early. In consequence, English secondary school teachers treat even 11 and 12 year olds as consisting of a small minority that matter and a large majority that do not really matter for educational purposes. For that reason, the poor results of 13 and 14 year olds in the IEA data may perhaps be yet another backwash effect of our extraordinary O and A-level examination system.

Prais has made a case: there is more vocational training for out-of-school youngsters in Germany than in the United Kingdom; the training reaches a higher standard and the cognitive achievements of the German formal school system are superior to ours. But what follows from that? Are we to believe that if we adopted German educational and training practices, we would eventually achieve Germany's level of output per worker? Prais never commits himself to so crude a theory of labour productivity. The most he says is that, while technical progress in the past has frequently done as much to deskill labour as to raise the demand for more skills, industrial success nowadays requires a skilled labour force. Perhaps, but who is to say that it is the higher German skill level that is called for and not the lower British one. No economist of education has ever successfully quantified the notion of required skill levels to achieve stated targets of economic growth. It follows that Prais' recommendations that we emulate Germany's system of training, if not education, rests on little more than an appeal to our emotions: since Germany is richer than we are, it must know something that we don't and that something *might* be its system of vocational training and its system of formal schooling.

I fully appreciate the work involved in comparing only two countries but I nevertheless insist that we cannot begin to take Prais' argument seriously without further comparisons, involving at least two or three more countries. Let us take another high growth country like Japan and ask what they do. Let us also look at a low-growth country like Italy and ask whether they have performed as poorly as we have in the field of training. All we have so far is a hypothesis confirmed by a sample of two.

Comments on Chapters 8–10
by Gareth Williams

It is easy and rather enjoyable to take up one of two extreme positions when discussing education and the economy. One is to draw attention to the fact that for several generations British economic performance appears to have been inferior to that of several of our competitors and to argue that since education is the main formal preparation for adult life of each generation, deficiencies in education must be responsible for the continuing mediocre performance. At the opposite extreme we may emphasise the heterogeneity of education and claim that its relationships with the economy are so manifold, so complex, so tenuous and so empirically untested that broad claims about education and economic performance are merely expressions of belief which tell us more about the protagonist's view of the world than about the world itself. Neither of these extremes is very helpful.

Many of the general points I would have wished to make are already contained in chapter 9 so I will content myself with some rather more detailed considerations of the interface between education and economic activity.

To draw an analogy with the study of medicine we need to move away from epidemiological models and towards clinical observation: or in this company perhaps I should say from the macroeconomic to the microeconomic – from theories of the national economy to the practices of employers. Professor Postlethwaite and Dr Prais offer us the hypothesis that the way we treat pupils in the bottom half of the academic achievement range has a significant effect on the performance of the economy. Their findings have been broadly familiar to people concerned with education policy for many years. One of the scandals of British education has long been the high proportion of people who leave school as soon as they can get away with it, never to enter an educational or training establishment again throughout their lives. Prais would give them specific vocational training from their early teenage years while Postlethwaite would drill them in algebra and geometry. I agree entirely with the proposition that there are advantages for all boys and girls in being good at number work and in learning a trade – so long as they are not left in a position of being unable or unwilling to do anything else if that skill should be superseded by technological progress or the fickleness of consumer demand. However, our task here is to consider *how* such deficiences in British education might affect our national economic performance. I would like to ask Prais if he can indicate observable mechanisms by which the superior craft training of German workers manifests itself in the performance of the German economy especially when he himself hints (p. 44) that it may not all be strictly necessary. If so, at what point between the current practices of Britain and Germany should we be aiming? To what extent can or should explicit needs of industries determine the content and quantity of vocational training? What if the combined needs of industry for young recruits amount to less than the number of young people coming on to the labour market each year? I would like to ask Postlethwaite to be specific about what less academic youngsters would be able to do better if they were better at algebra and geometry or if they had mastered a craft? British employers in practice, whatever they say in public speeches, are remarkably ambiguous on the matter (see [1] for a useful review of research findings). Many studies have shown that they are not much impressed by school leavers who have done subjects like technical drawing and commerce and typing. I did one myself a few years ago and found that employers seem to prefer school leavers who have qualifications in traditional subjects such as English and mathematics [3,4]. But when we pursue the matter further and ask what young people actually do in their early jobs it transpires that they make little use of the specific skills involved in these two subjects.

Secretaries find it useful to be able to correct (tactfully) their employers' spelling and grammar and trainees for technical jobs (usually well above the median of the ability range) find some mathematics useful. Apart from this what most people actually do at work bears little relationship to what they have learned at school. With few exceptions this applies right up to the level of a degree. If, therefore, employers want recruits who are good at English and mathematics this must imply either that these skills are proxies for attributes that are really useful at work or that ability to master English and/or mathematics entails an ability to acquire and use information in ways that are useful in employment. What employers really seem to be impressed by are conventional modes of dress, speech and behaviour and a critical attitude that nonetheless accepts the basic ethos of the firm or organisation.

Whether we accept such evidence as indicators of the relationship between education and the economic performance of individuals depends in large part on whether employers know why they are looking for particular qualities in their young recruits. There are some reasons for believing that often they do not. As already noted, many employees do not make use of mathematics and English they have learned at school even when they are selected for proficiency at these subjects. Another shred of evidence pointing in the same direction is that few employers keep personnel records that permit them to check whether the assumptions they make when recruiting young people are borne out in subsequent work performance. In many firms the process of recruitment is separated from the employment of people once they are recruited and there is little feedback of information from the production managers to recruitment managers. It does not appear even that employers are particularly likely to set salaries at levels which reflect shortages of particular skills. Despite the apparent persistent shortage of engineers and technologists their salaries and career prospects tend to lag behind those of accountants and salesmen. I am rather surprised that a conference on the subject of education and economic performance does not have a single session devoted to the subject of education and salaries. While individual salaries are obviously influenced by other factors as well as individual economic performance there is little doubt that differences in anticipated lifetime earnings are a powerful motivating factor for young people in secondary and further education [2,5]. I hope that one outcome of this conference might be a call for further study of earnings–education relationships of the type that have been carried out in considerable detail in the United States National Labour Market Surveys.

This kind of evidence points in a familiar direction. If we are seeking educational causes of deficiencies in the British economy we should look first at the formation of attitudes and competences of those who fill leading managerial positions. Here, the list of differences from other countries is well known. Few other economically advanced countries have a private sector of secondary education so sharply distinguished from the education of the mass of the population; none encourage the most able young people to specialize so narrowly at such an early age; few put such an emphasis on academic science as opposed to applied science and technology and few have had such a marked tendency for the best graduates to enter the civil service or remain in academic life, thus slanting a large part of undergraduate education in the interest of such occupational groups.

I do not want to appear to be complacent about the way British education has treated lower than average academic achievers. But the motivation for reform should come from the needs of the pupils themselves and not because on the evidence available it is likely to do much to stimulate national economic growth. The growing problems of drug addiction and football hooliganism are better indicators of deficiency than the nebulous link between generalised performance in mathematics tests and generalised performance at work.

However, I should like to raise a few questions about Professor Postlethwaite's figures. I do not want to dispute the figures themselves. I am sufficiently old fashioned in my approach to social sciences to believe that anything that can be quantified has some reality (which is not at all the same thing as believing that if anything is real it can be quantified). However there are one or two interesting features of the 'Bottom Half'. One is the will o' the wisp aspect of Germany and Japan. Germany does not appear in table 8.1 – neither Germany nor Japan appear in table 8.2. Since these are the two countries likely to be uppermost in the minds of our readers we ought to know why.

Turning to chart 8.3, which is the most useful in the paper being the only one based on post comprehensive secondary education data, it really is difficult to know what to make of this information without knowing the identities of countries E and F. If they should turn out to be Germany and Japan I shall be impressed. Otherwise I must express some doubts on the significance of the differences on which we are invited to reflect. Again the sceptic in one wonders why Country A and Country C have been omitted from table 8.2.

One final specific comment on chapter 8 is educational rather than statistical. Presumably Postlethwaite does not intend us to take too literally his claim that there should be a one-to-one relationship of the examination to what was to have been learned. This would surely imply telling examinees the answers beforehand and asking them to remember them.

What we surely want is a correspondence between (i) what is likely to be worth knowing in adult life, (ii) what is to be learned, (iii) the certification that it has been learned and (iv) the ability to use that learning in a variety of circumstances later in life. The steps that are missing in Postlethwaite's paper are the first and last. It is not easy to show that the ability to pass examinations is the same as the ability to perform well in adult tasks. And there does not seem to be much agreement, except at the most banal level of generality, about what curricula are likely to be useful in adult life. Of course we may take the view that it doesn't much matter what pupils learn so long as they all learn the same thing but we cannot ignore the evidence that many European countries have been trying to decentralise and diversify their curricula for many years.

We could usefully devote some time to a consideration of whether from an economic point of view there is a case for greater centralization of the curriculum as both Prais and Postlethwaite believe. If so who should be involved in formulating it? In order to initiate the discussion I will say that I believe employers should be brought into the process of curriculum determination at national and local level but they should be asked to base their advice on hard evidence of their own experiences in employing school-leavers and not the kind of rhetoric that sounds good at CBI conferences. I suggest this not because I think that employers will propose curricula very different from groups of professionally responsible teachers. But the process of thinking about what school-leavers really ought to know might encourage employers to think seriously about who it is they really want to employ. And if they know what qualities they really want they might make better use of the skills of their young employees and start giving the right labour market signals.

References

[1] Gordon, Alan, *How to Choose School Leavers for Jobs*, Aldershot, Gower, 1983.
[2] Pissarides, Christopher, 'From school to university: the demand for post compulsory education in Britain', *Economic Journal*, vol. 92, September 1982.
[3] Reid, Eileen, 'Managers and young employees', *Policy Studies*, vol. 1, part 3, 1981.
[4] Williams, Gareth, 'Reflections on the responses of employers to educational qualifications', *Policy Studies*, vol. 2, part 2, 1981.
[5] Williams, Gareth and Gordon, Alan, 'Perceived earnings functions and ex ante rates of return to post compulsory education in England', *Higher Education*, vol. 10, no. 2, 1981.

Comments on Chapters 9 and 10
by Maurice Kogan

Chapters 9 and 10 address the related themes of how far educational values have been hospitable to notions of national redemption through enhanced productivity, and the extent to which the education system could respond to demands for change.

The chapters, taken together, imply that we have to think in terms of congruence or conflict between three cultures. The first is that of what Maclure calls 'the larger social and cultural priorities'. Education is, he maintains, subordinate to them. I assume that he includes the economic priority of productivity. Secondly, there are the academic cultures which, as William Taylor shows so well, emerged in the second half of the nineteenth century as strongly monodisciplinary rather than synoptic. They were also, however, critical of the ethos of industrial society. And thirdly, less explicit in the papers, is what I would call the internal logic of schools and schooling.

Whenever social scientists see two ideas, let alone three, they assume that there must be conflict. But civilised people can hold two or three ideas in their minds at once. In this spirit it is appropriate to supplement the themes analysed by Taylor and Maclure by advancing the notion that secondary education has an internal logic which is incorporated into quite powerful institutions. Whilst it is possible, as does Maclure, to enumerate the different forces from the outside that operate on the school, the permeability of schools remains questionable.

As one talks to teachers and visits schools it is difficult not to be impressed by the way in which teachers express views of pupil development which derive from working with them rather than from exogenous demands and assumptions. The notion of individual pupil development is strongly present in British secondary education. Although progressive educators might maintain that the former grammar schools eschewed effective dimensions of education in deference to pressure to get passes in GCE or School Certificates, the picture drawn of the sixth form in the Crowther Report, roseate as it was, was essentially that of humanistic individualism. Now individualism, deeply ingrained into the notion of the British progressive primary school and secondary education as well, has obviously been strongly modified by the growing power of egalitarian ideology in education: William Taylor describes this well. There has been a move from notions grounded perhaps in developmental psychology towards those deriving from critical sociology, sociology of knowledge, and sociology concerned with the distribution of life chances. Individual development has yielded ground at some levels to the egalitarian theme as, for example, when the more radical local authorities insist on changes in the curriculum in favour of minorities.

So far this does not constitute a logic of secondary education. But there is one. By logic I mean a propensity to see secondary education as being worthwhile for its own sake. It is concerned with the processes through which schools work with pupils from the age of 11–16 or 11–18. These are assumed to have validity in themselves, because those are years to be lived to the full, and because they are concerned with individual development rather than with exogenous demands. Each style of education has its own assumptions about the needs of its pupils and finds it difficult to accept the assumptions of the neighbouring stages.

At the same time, however, the schools have been the recipient of the disciplinary cultures which have percolated through the public examinations at the end of secondary education and the demands set up by those selecting pupils for higher education. The schools are at constant war with those who impose these requirements on them and the delights of freedom in the first three years of secondary education, which some, however, would prefer to regard as somewhat inchoate, give way to what is undoubtedly the pressure cooking at least for the abler pupils in the last two years of the five year course. Taken together these two cultures might be inhospitable to productivity values.

Educators have assumed, however, that broadly based education makes people more productive than happy. Taylor draws on Dore in noting how employers in higher education are by no means certain about the correspondence between instrumentally connoted education and their best employees. They want good chaps. They are not much interested in the constituents of higher education curriculum. They are concerned that graduate recruits have good A-levels, but are not terribly worried about the subjects taken or what taking those subjects means. Japanese employers also prefer able recruits without much anxiety about what they did at university. By contrast, some of the least productive countries in the world are extremely tight lipped in formulating curricula in both secondary and higher education which will lead to all of the social and economic virtues.

By contrast with what the school already advances by way of educational values and academic disciplines, the culture of productivity seems far less secure.

Returning now to the school, the indigenous culture leads to specifics. The way schools are organised demonstrates pretty clearly how authority is distributed and to what ends. Look at an organisation chart and you will be able to see the balance of power struck between work on the curriculum and work on the pastoral aspects of the school. Within the curriculum one can detect the balance between specific skills training and more general and attitudinal development, premised on what Taylor quotes as being 'an initiation into a worthwhile form of life.'

Curriculum may be strongly influenced by external examinations. These may make schools less adaptive to the needs of the labour market than higher education which does after all give many of its highest prizes to technology and science. The number of product related degrees increases each year.

By contrast, the school is a boundaried institution. It is not at all clear that pressures from the centre will affect its way of working. We just do not know what are the mechanisms through which influences reach the school. At the grossest level, of course, change can be directed. Abolishing the grammar schools meant that the power of grammar school type teachers was reduced. That's pretty obvious. Changing a grouped School Certificate into single subject GCEs changed the nature of sixth forms and loosened up the whole area of 16–19 year old education.

But having said this, one cannot wriggle off the hook which Stuart Maclure baited at the beginning of chapter 10. Schools are set in a general culture. Traditional forms of education became mixed with individualistic and hedonic forms. Recent movements towards egalitarianism were not all internally generated.

Now for the first time, however, we have radical government approaches such as those described by Stuart Maclure. Specific grants are back. Maclure is surely right to say that inducements such as these can only succeed if they are built upon some kind of normative consensus and the building up of the policy networks and communities and coalitions. That consensus, however, must be built on respecting what I have described as the many cultures that affect the schools. The MSC in particular needs to make a stronger intellectual effort to understand what are the indigenous cultures and organisations of the institutions which they seek to influence. Heroic ministers can cause massive changes if they try, but I am suggesting here that the changes should be those deriving from the eclecticism of Joseph, with his coat of many colours, rather than Moses with his tablets of stone.

Comments on Chapters 8–10
by David Stanton

I want to begin by deliberately focusing on one theme that appears in both chapters 9 and 10 even if in a slightly different form. Taylor's parable from Scotland is a clear warning that no progress will be made in a discussion of how the education system responds to change if the issue is forced into a simple two-dimensional framework. Simple solutions imposed from the centre are rarely going to result in improvement. This is also a message I draw from Maclure's chapter. I agree with this view even to the extent that I want to suggest that both authors have tended to assume that change is usually a matter of a single discrete modification. Of more interest, because it is usually the engine of most institutional adaptation, is the process of small changes at the margin.

This means that I am not going to discuss the large and important issues which the historical perspective of both chapters highlights. I would like instead to concentrate on the links between the education system and the labour market. To Maclure's list of the pressures that determine what happens in schools (page 114) I would like to suggest adding the demands of the labour market. Ensuring that people have the correct schooling, within the resources available, to enable them to work, is a necessary function of the education system; without such a background the other objectives of education cannot be achieved.

In certain parts of the education system there is clear evidence of change taking place in response to changes in the labour market, and little of it is the result of large forces of history. Where people have choices and where their choices are recorded there have been signs that pressure to change within education is largely the result of people voting with their feet. For example, the awareness of new technology and the need for numerate manpower is clearly reflected in the growth in people taking A-level mathematics and science. The table below shows how there has been an overall growth in numbers but a disproportionate growth in maths and science.

Numbers with O level passes

	1977	1982	% change
Mathematics	48,269	64,833	34.3
Science and Technology	139,274	175,580	26.1
Arts	128,965	132,935	3.1
Total	361,323	416,361	15.2

This trend, which reflects the growing demands arising from new technology, is also reflected in Higher Education. For example, the ratio of applicants to places in electronic engineering is nearly 3:1 and the A-level price for a place has recently risen faster than it has for other courses.

The examples quoted do not mean that the education system responds immediately to such pressures. An increase in applications to study a particular subject does not translate immediately into extra resources – nor should it since some built-in checks are necessary for efficiency. But when resources are re-allocated it is in response to these pressures.

It is not so obvious how these examples are relevant to the school system up to 16. There is little direct choice except for the minority who take GCE O-levels and to a lesser extent CSE. For the majority there is little information on which to make the limited choices that are available. Prais's comparison of the education standards in Germany and England emphasises how little measurement of education performance occurs in this country. I would like to suggest for discussion that more measurement and greater availability of information would help to facilitate the small changes that in the end are more important than any attempt to achieve large changes in direction. A better idea of how different parts of the education system achieve one of their goals – an education that enhances the employment prospects of school leavers – will help to ensure that resources are reallocated more efficiently.

Summary of the Discussion

The conference discussed the links between education and economic performance. Work by economists in the 1960s, which related individuals' earnings to their 'investment' in education (measured by years of schooling) appeared to indicate a strong causal link between the volume of education provision and economic performance. This conclusion was reinforced by international comparative studies which highlighted the conjuncture of relatively high productivity and long schooling periods in the United States.

But economists are now more wary of asserting any simple relationship between economic performance and the quantity of education experienced by the labour force as measured by years of schooling. For example, recent research has tended to emphasise the role of education as a 'positional good'. Further international comparative work at the National Institute has shown that labour productivity is significantly lower in Britain than in other European countries, despite similarities in the average number of years spent in school per head of the labour force.

Might such similarities in the years of schooling therefore disguise distinctive British weaknesses in the quality of education provision? If so, what are they, and how have they affected economic performance?

In response to the evidence on certain educational output measures presented by Prais and Postlethwaite, there was a wide measure of agreement that the British education system was not 'doing well by' the bottom half of the ability range. However, there was also much dispute both about the significance of Postlethwaite's results and also of the wider implications of the findings, if valid, for economic performance.

Could it be said, for example, that the British results were significantly worse than those achieved in other countries in any strict statistical sense? Or were the results simply picking up different emphases in the school curricula in different countries – although the implications of this were not carried over into the discussion of the British school curriculum.

Some scepticism was also expressed on the significance of the Prais–Postlethwaite results, if true, for economic performance. In the same way that the large volume of training in Germany might represent a degree of over-provision, might not the high levels of educational attainment observed in some other countries be an example of over-provision in relation to the needs of the economy? On the other hand, it was suggested than an education sytem which apparently failed to equip a large proportion of its graduates with certain very basic numeracy skills was not serving either their personal needs or those of the economy at large efficiently.

The conference then discussed what might be done to improve the educational experience and attainments especially of the bottom half, and what were the main obstacles to change.

There was also discussion of the pressures and incentives acting on the education system and the processes by which the needs of the economy were articulated and transmitted. On the demand side, conflicting views were heard on the effectiveness of labour market signals in influencing pupils' choices at the secondary level. Several speakers argued that the signals were highly confused and that employers needed to think more strategically about recruitment policies and to articulate their likely future requirements more clearly, especially at the level of local labour markets. There was scope for more active participation here by local employers' organisations, similar to that of the Chambers of Commerce in Germany. It was by no means clear that employers were demanding more young people with technical or vocational qualifications from school; instead, they tended to emphasise the importance of cognitive skills and certain behavioural traits, memorably summarised by one speaker as 'biddability'.

Others suggested that where effective choice could be exercised and where relevant information was available, for example in respect of pupils' choice of A-level subjects, significant changes had occurred in the pattern of demand in response to labour market signals. Recent initiatives by the DES to publicise information on the early labour market experience of university graduates by subject area were generally welcomed. However, the opportunity to exercise choice in public education (other than to withdraw to the private sector) was very limited below the upper secondary level, and relevant information on performance of schools in the primary and lower secondary sectors was hard to come by. Finally, the conference was warned not to deceive itself: improved information alone would not necessarily lead to an increase in total employment.

On the supply side, it was recognised that the education system in England and Wales is very highly decentralised. In particular, decisions on curriculum content were the responsibility of the 30,000 or so head teachers employed by over 100 autonomous local education authorities. Central government leverage on the system was very limited since its contributions to the support of educational expenditures were almost exclusively channelled through block grants to local authorities. Allocation of resources within this system took place in response to a wide variety of outside pressures, with which those emanating from the world of work must compete. Some speakers felt that the attempt to accommodate these diverse pressures has already overloaded the schools curriculum.

In principle, employers' requirements could be transmitted both through their participation in administrative processes and through the qualifications which were sought in recruiting employees from the school system. However, recent attempts to increase the influence of employers at local level had been hamstrung by changes in the local authority committee structure. Following the 1972 DES circular, non-elected members, including representatives of local trade and industry, had been introduced to local education committees, but the role of the education committee itself had been weakened by a tendency to shift key decisions on educational expenditure to the policy and resources committee which consisted only of elected members. A current policy initiative which, it was clearly hoped, would increase the responsiveness of education provision to the needs of the economy was the proposal to increase parental representation on school governing bodies. Several speakers sounded a note of caution on this. In particular it was pointed out that there is considerable diversity of view in society concerning the relative weight to be attached to the needs of the world of work and of academic competence on the one hand, and on the other to what might be called the 'socialising' aspects of school experience; this diversity would inevitably be reflected in the views of parent governors.

Pressures from the world of work appeared to be transmitted quite quickly and efficiently to the non-advanced further education (NAFE) sector and found reflection in the entry standards required. But because such a small proportion of the 16-plus age group proceed to further education in Britain, these standards were not a strong influence on the secondary school curriculum, in contrast to the position in Germany, where a very large proportion of the age group studied at the *Berufschule*.

The conference also discussed the capacity of the education system to respond to shortages of teachers in particular subjects. It was noted that there had been enormous resistance to allowing the pay of mathematics and science teachers, who have been persistently in short supply, to increase beyond what is possible within the Burnham scale structure.

Worries were also expressed about school management. For example, it was doubted whether head teachers in the public sector were in a sufficiently strong position to dismiss incompetent teachers. One speaker also wondered whether the responsiveness of the school system might be increased if head teachers' posts were made non-tenured. However, there was clearly a danger that this might simply make the system more responsive to what were described as short-term fads and fashions.

Perhaps recognising the truth of remarks that the school system has certain very strong indigenous cultural traditions which made it highly resistant to outside pressure, some speakers recommended a significant shift in the financing of education expenditure to increase the leverage of central government. Others doubted whether the DES would be prepared to acccept the responsibilities of leadership and some felt that the Manpower Services Commission was a potentially more powerful vehicle for encouraging change. It was felt that d'Iribarne's description of the French vocational training reforms, which he saw as a way round the prejudices of a monolithic educational system which was out of touch with the needs of the economy, could also be applied to some recent British initiatives. Their purpose was to influence the Commission both through the technical and vocational education initiative (TVEI) and through the new arrangements for funding the NAFE sector. However, previous attempts to introduce a distinctive 'technical' stream into British secondary education had not been successful and some felt that the survival of TVEI once specific funding had been withdrawn was highly problematic, especially in view of the relatively costly nature of its courses.

Index